STUDIO ONE FOR ENGINEERS AND PRODUCERS

quick**PRO**
guides

STUDIO ONE
FOR
ENGINEERS
AND
PRODUCERS

William Edstrom, Jr.

Hal Leonard Books
An Imprint of Hal Leonard Corporation

Published in 2013 by Hal Leonard Books
An Imprint of Hal Leonard Corporation
7777 West Bluemound Road
Milwaukee, WI 53213

Trade Book Division Editorial Offices
33 Plymouth St., Montclair, NJ 07042

Printed in the United States of America

Book design by Adam Fulrath
Book composition by Kristina Rolander

Library of Congress Cataloging-in-Publication Data

Edstrom, William, Jr.
 Studio One for engineers and producers / William Edstrom, Jr.
     pages cm. -- (Quick Pro Guides)
 Includes index.
 ISBN 978-1-4768-0602-0
1. Studio One (Computer file) 2. Digital audio editors. I. Title. II. Title: Studio 1 for engineers and producers.
 ML74.4.S79E37 2013
 781.3'4536--dc23
                                   2012045993

www.halleonardbooks.com

CONTENTS

PART II: STUDIO ONE PROFESSIONAL EDITING

Chapter 5

Chapter 6

Chapter 7

Chapter 8

PART III: STUDIO ONE PROFESSIONAL MIXING

Chapter 9

Chapter 10

Chapter 11

Chapter 12

Chapter 13

PART IV: STUDIO ONE PROFESSIONAL MASTERING AND RELEASING

Chapter 14

Chapter 15

PREFACE

If you are reading this book, you most likely have some degree of proficiency with modern recording software and are now getting started with Studio One. I have written this book to provide concise, direct answers to questions you might have as you work on your first projects in Studio One. Whether you come from Avid Pro Tools, Apple Logic, Cakewalk SONAR, Steinberg Cubase, Cockos Reaper, MOTU Digital Performer, Apple GarageBand, or another DAW you will recognize that Studio One is built on the same basic concepts as most other DAWs.

As you transition from other systems, you will find that some familiar tools work differently, are named differently, or are presented in new ways. *Studio One for Engineers and Producers* will help you understand how Studio One works, so you can make the transition quickly and efficiently. In this book I focus on accessing common and advanced tools that you need as a producer or engineer.

The videos on the companion DVD-ROM are an essential complement to the text. The video tutorials clarify some things that are easier to show than to tell. In addition, I expand on some of the advanced topics that didn't fit within the limitations of the text.

ACKNOWLEDGMENTS

I would like to thank the team at PreSonus that somehow decided the world needed another DAW. Studio One has become my favorite canvas for musical experiments. PreSonus has been incredibly open and welcoming to me as both an author and a customer. Thanks for being gracious hosts in Baton Rouge and at NAMM: Rick Naqvi, Jonathan Hillman, Brad Zell, Wolfgang Kundrus, Matthias Juwan, Bob Tudor, Jim Odom, and all the rest of the team.

Thanks to Asa and Antony at Groove 3 for getting me started and seeing me as an expert. Thanks to Scott Fritz at Stranded on a Planet for inspiration and demo tunes on my early projects.

Special thanks to the power users on the PreSonus forum. LMike, TheMuzic, and Motoko are among many who set the tone for the most helpful and friendly user community I have encountered online.

Thanks to my developmental editor, Bill Gibson, who thought I could write books and then taught me how. Thank you to Jessica Burr, the project editor of this book, for getting the manuscript in order for publishing. Also, thank you to copy editor Patty Hammond for making my words make sense.

A big thank-you to Andrew Edstrom, my college-student son, who assisted with formatting, proofreading, preparing demo tracks, and generally keeping me on track during the summer. Thanks to Toma, my younger son, for being a constant source of love and entertainment. Finally, thanks to my wife, Mari, for the many hours spent helping me with the final markups and for her endless support and love.

PART I: STUDIO ONE
PROFESSIONAL RECORDING

Chapter 1
GETTING STARTED

A Brief History of Studio One

In 2006, Wolfgang Kundrus, Mattias Juwan, and a small team of developers came together in Hamburg, Germany, to build a DAW from scratch. PreSonus Audio Electronics—a company in Baton Rouge, Louisiana, which at the time was better known for making audio interfaces, mic preamps, and compressors—took notice. Ultimately, PreSonus purchased the Hamburg operation, which became the PreSonus software development team. The first product this team released was Capture, an application designed for capturing multitrack recordings of live shows with the PreSonus StudioLive digital mixer. The second product was Studio One.

The public beta of Studio One debuted in 2009. Early reviewers praised its easy workflow but were critical of its limited feature set. Over time it gained enthusiastic users, particularly musicians, producers, and songwriters who were doing their own engineering and enjoyed using a DAW that didn't interrupt creative flow.

The second version of Studio One, aptly named Studio One 2, launched in the fall of 2011 with a core feature set to compete with the major DAWs. Its off-the-shelf integration with Celemony Melodyne pitch editing surpassed anything available in competing products. Studio One 2 included many requested features such as Folder Tracks, Event FX, track freezing (called Track Transform), tab-to-transient, audio warping (called Audio Bend), silence removal, audio quantizing, and hundreds of other new tweaks and features.

Since the release of Studio One 2, the number of users has increased dramatically. Users coming from other systems are often lured by Studio One's workflow, sound quality, and Melodyne integration. PreSonus continues to introduce new features and updates, continuing the evolution of Studio One.

Key Features

This is a list of key features in Studio One Professional:

- Is Windows and Mac compatible
- Has full 64-bit or 32-bit operation

- Has audio-recording capabilities limited only by computer capabilities
- Has comprehensive audio editing tools
- Supports VST effects on Windows and Mac
- Supports AU effects on OS X
- Has 32 included effects
- Has 64-bit or 32-bit operation
- Is compatible with most audio interfaces
- Supports ASIO on Windows
- Supports Audio Units on OS X
- Has configurable keyboard shortcuts
- Has four virtual instruments: Presence, Mojito, SampleOne, and Impact
- Supports VSTi effects on Windows and Mac
- Supports AU instruments on Mac
- Can record an unlimited number of Instrument Tracks
- Has pitch editing using Melodyne
- Has audio timing, editing, and quantizing with Audio Bend
- Has an integrated Project page for mastering, CD authoring, and digital releases
- Has file bit depths of 16-, 24-, and 32-bit float
- Has a Song and Project version-control system to save in-progress versions for easy rollback

Figure 1-1

- Can do a full undo during the session
- Has integrated support for creating MP3 files
- Has basic video support for aligning audio to video
- Includes PreSonus Exchange, to share and access presets, loops, and extensions
- Has a simple, integrated upgrade mechanism
- Has the Macro Toolbar to create custom interactions
- Has easy mapping of hardware knobs and faders to onscreen controls using Control Link
- Has practical license management with no dongles
- Has effective Audio Track timestretching based on Zplane Élastique
- Can automatically match loops to the project tempo
- Has Browser view with drag-and-drop for instruments, loops, presets, effects, and more
- Has Track Transform to "freeze" both Audio and Instrument Tracks

Figure 1-2

What Doesn't Studio One Have?

At the time of writing, some features were not part of Studio One. This is not to say that Studio One should or ever will have any of these features. I am just pointing out some features that other DAWs have that the new users commonly ask about.

For most of these features, you will need to use third-party plug-ins or other tools if these are essential for you. Check the Studio One website (Figure 1-1) to see if some of these have been added since publication of this book.

Here are some of the missing features.

Figure 1-3

Tempo Detection

Studio One can easily manipulate tempo, but you will need to figure out the original file tempo by using another third-party tool or matching the Tempo Track to your audio manually. I use a free tool from MixMeister called BPM Analyzer (Figure 1-2).

There are also numerous tap tempo calculators for iOS. I use one called BPM from Thumb Labs (Figure 1-3).

Figure 1-4

Step Sequencer

Studio One doesn't include a step sequencer. A drum instrument, Impact, is included, but it offers drum sounds, not programming.

There are many third-party drum instruments with sequencers than can fill this need. Here are a few popular choices. Maschine from Native Instruments (Figure 1-4) is one of the most popular, full-featured products that include cool hardware integration.

Drumaxx is an alternative from Image-Line Software that features modeled drum sounds and a capable sequencer (Figure 1-5).

Figure 1-5

Block Arrangement

Cubase and Reason have tools to define song sections in order to experiment with different arrangements. In Studio One, you can select and move full blocks of song sections with the Range tool and move them around with drag-and-drop. At this point Studio One doesn't have any sort of block arrangement view or similar tools.

Score Editor

Cubase, SONAR, Pro Tools, and Logic all have score editors. Although Studio One does not have a score editor, it is simple to export MIDI files, which can then be imported into other score editors.

Figure 1-6

MIDI FX

SONAR and Cubase support MIDI plug-ins to process the MIDI between tracks, controls, and virtual instruments. Studio One does have Input Quantize but has no MIDI plug-in support.

Clip Launch

Ableton Live and SONAR have views allowing you to play with loops for live performance or composing. Studio One does not contain this feature.

Figure 1-7

Bit Bridge

Logic and SONAR allow you to run older 32-bit plug-ins while in 64-bit mode using a type of adapter called a "bit bridge." Studio One does not have an included bit bridge solution.

PreSonus doesn't openly support third-party bit bridge software. However, some users report good results using the third-party jBridge (Figure 1-6).

Unless absolutely necessary, I would stay away from bit bridge software and run plug-ins that are written for the environment you are running.

Figure 1-8

Loudness Maximizer

Studio One has a comprehensive multiband dynamics effects processor and a capable limiter that can be used for mastering. However, it doesn't have the type of loudness maximizer typical in modern mastering. To get this functionality, you can use a plug-in like iZotope Ozone (Figure 1-7), Waves L2 (Figure 1-8), or Slate Digital FG-X (Figure 1-9).

Inline MIDI Editor

There is no way to edit individual Notes in the Arrange view. What you see in the Arrange view is an Instrument Part. An Instrument Part is a container for Notes. To edit the notes, double-click on the Instrument Track to open the Music Editor.

MIDI Event List

Figure 1-9

Unlike what you find in other systems, there is no event list for MIDI notes. All note editing is done in the Music Editor, which is essentially a piano-roll view.

Compatibility

Studio One has modest minimum system requirements.

Mac

- OS X 10.6.8 or later
- Intel Core 2 Duo processor
- 2 GB of RAM (4 GB recommended)

Windows

- Windows 32-bit or 64-bit, XP, Vista, 7, or 8
- Intel Core 2 Duo processor (AMD X2 and X4 are also supported)
- 2 GB of RAM (4 GB recommended)

Other Requirements

- 1,280 × 768 minimum display resolution
- DVD-ROM drive
- 20 GB of hard drive space

My Recommendations

If you are planning to run Studio One as a 64-bit application, I suggest you have 8 GB or more of RAM. If you have 4 GB or less of RAM, you will probably get better results sticking with a 32-bit version of Studio One. If you are running Windows, I suggest you use Windows 7 or higher because these versions have much more robust support for digital audio.

Versions and Licensing

Studio One is available in multiple versions:

Studio One Artist. Artist has the core DAW functionality but has no Projects page, fewer effects, and no support for third-party VST/AU plug-ins.

Studio One Producer. Producer is similar to the Artist version but includes support for third-party effects and instruments.

Studio One Professional. Studio One Professional is the full version of Studio One. It includes additional effects, integrated mastering, Melodyne integration, SoundCloud integration, and full 64-bit operation. You will get the most out of this book if you have Studio One Professional.

Abbreviations

To make keyboard shortcuts more succinct, I use the following abbreviations: "Cmd" for "Command," "Ctrl" for "Control," and "Opt" for "Option."

Mac Versus Windows Platforms

Studio One on a Mac works similarly to the way it does in Windows and is a fantastic music-production system on either platform. Here is an explanation of the few minor differences.

Options and Preferences

The Options dialog box is accessed from Studio One > Preferences on a Mac. The same dialog box is accessed from Studio One > Options in Windows. It is the same thing but the menu location is different. For this book I will either show both options or just refer to it as the Options dialog box. You can also access it via Cmd + Comma (Mac) or Ctrl + Comma (Windows).

Command and Control

In this book, I present both Mac and Windows shortcut versions in the format Mac / Windows. For example, the keyboard shortcut to export a mixdown is Cmd + E / Ctrl + E.

Notes for Mac Users

Studio One makes extensive use of right-click context menus. Long-term Mac users know that Ctrl-click is used for context menus just like a right-click is used in Windows. For brevity's sake, I will say "right-click," but you can substitute Ctrl-click in most of those cases.

In Studio One, the function keys F1 through F10 are mapped to show or hide the most common views in Studio One. For example, F3 opens and closes the Console view, while F5 opens and closes the Browser. On the Mac, the function keys F1 through F10 are assigned to system functions like volume control and brightness adjustment by default. This means you need to hold down the Fn key in combination with the function keys to access the Studio One view commands (Fn + F3 to open and close the Console view).

I recommend you switch this preference in OS X to allow direct access to the Studio One view commands without having to hold down the Fn key. You can find the setting in Preferences > Keyboard on your Mac.

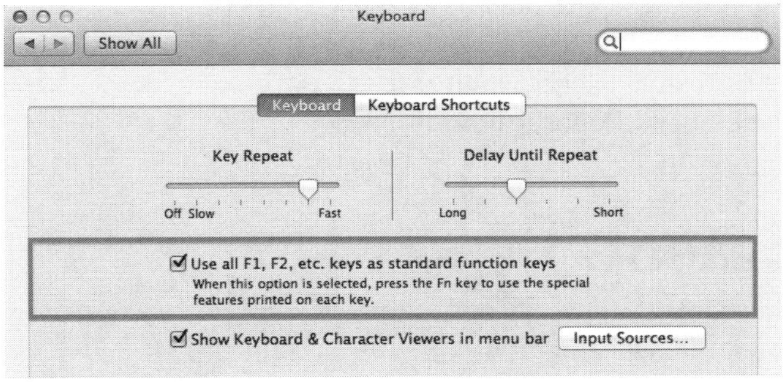

Figure 1-10

In the rest of this book, I will assume you have OS X configured this way.

Installing Studio One

Studio One is easy to install either from the DVD or by downloading from the PreSonus website. It is essential to set up a user account with PreSonus because all updates and software activations require it. Activations are handled through a challenge-response system, so no hardware dongles are necessary.

License Activations

Studio One includes five activations per serial number. This means you can install and activate Studio One up to five times. For convenience you can run Studio One on more than one computer, but by the license it should be run on only one computer at a time. If you switch your computer hardware and run out of activations, you can contact PreSonus support and have your activations reset.

It is possible to activate Studio One either online or offline. To activate it online just select that option when Studio One starts. There you can enter your PreSonus user ID and password along with the license key.

To activate a device offline, copy the license file from your PreSonus My Software account to a USB drive. Insert the USB drive into the target machine and locate the license file. Dropping the license file on the activation screen completes offline activation.

32-Bit and 64-Bit Versions

For Mac OS X users the same installation can be run in 32-bit or 64-bit mode. To toggle this, right-click on the Studio One application file and select Get Info. If "Open in 32-bit mode" is checked, then Studio One will open in 32-bit. Otherwise it will open in 64-bit.

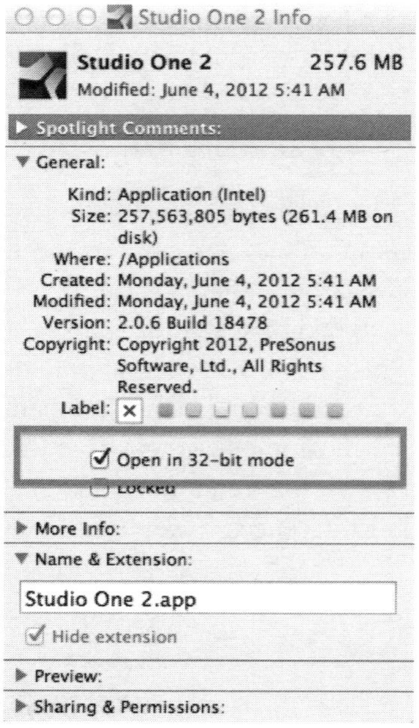

Upgrading

PreSonus releases frequent updates to Studio One to correct bugs and add features between major releases. If your computer is connected to the Internet, Studio One checks for new versions on startup and allows you to easily update. You can also check for new updates at any time by going to Help > Check for Updates.

If your computer running Studio One is offline, then you can always download the latest version to another device from your PreSonus user account under My Software and transfer it to your studio computer with a USB drive.

Figure 1-11

Additional Content

Studio One comes with several gigabytes of loops, sounds, and software. If you purchased a physical copy of Studio One, this is all contained on the disc. If not, it can easily be installed from the Studio One Installation dialog box (Studio One > Studio One Installation).

Click on "Install content from PreSonus user account," then select the content to download and install.

If your computer is not connected to the Internet, you can download the additional content from your PreSonus My Software account and transfer the files via a USB drive to your studio computer for installation.

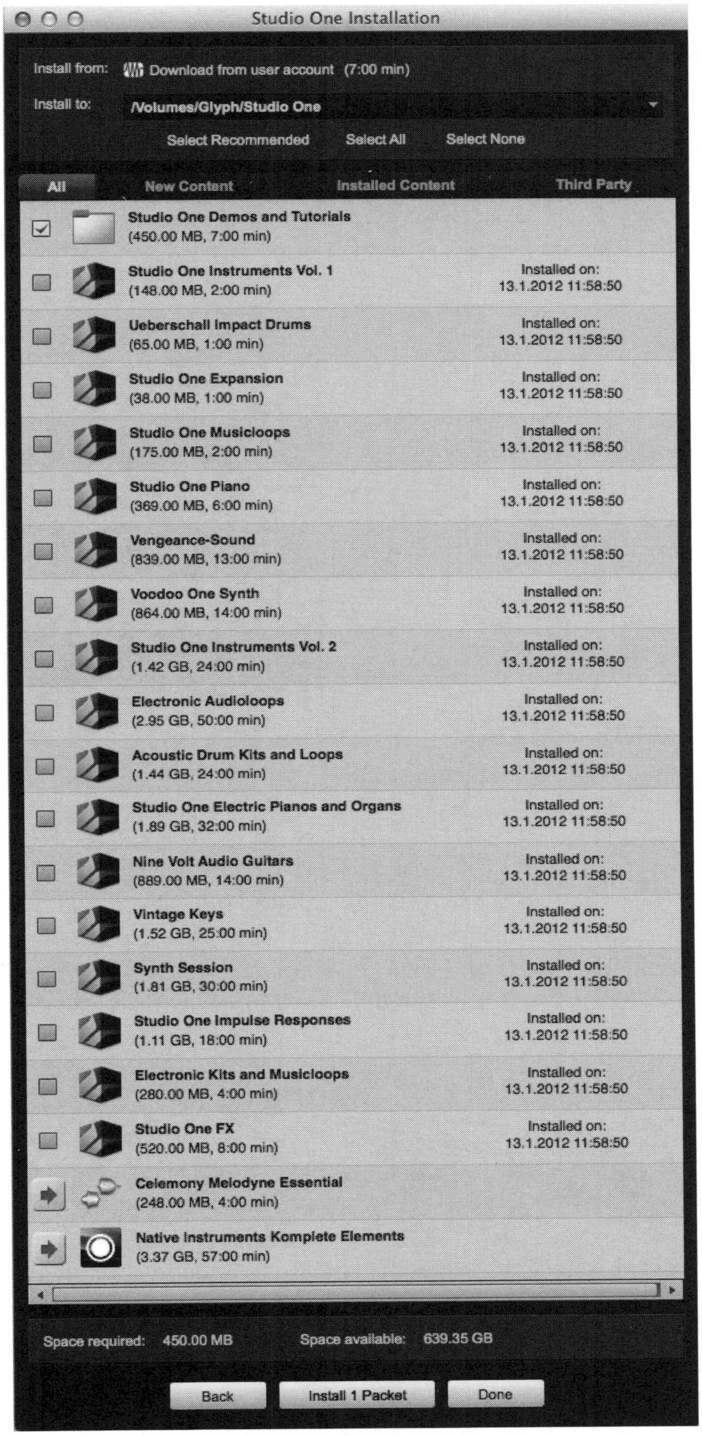

Figure 1-12

Extensions

You can add features to Studio One with extensions. These are managed at Studio One > Studio One Extensions. Extensions for SoundCloud and PreSonus Exchange are installed and enabled by default. Additional extensions are available from PreSonus Exchange and can be easily installed from the Browser.

Macro Toolbar

The Macro Toolbar extension is particularly useful. It's a fully customizable toolbar that lets you organize any Studio One action into groups of buttons. Each macro can contain numerous steps, allowing you to string actions together to automate repetitive tasks. Macros can be assigned to buttons on the Toolbar, keyboard shortcuts, or even MIDI continuous controller (MIDI CC) events from your controller.

This is an important feature that allows you to tailor Studio One to the type of work you are doing. It can dramatically increase your productivity when you are faced with doing repetitive tasks.

PreSonus Exchange

PreSonus Exchange is an online system that allows you to download and exchange sounds, loops, presets, and extensions with other users. It is available directly in the Studio One Browser.

If your studio computer is not online, you can download Exchange content from another computer through a web version of Exchange (Figure 1-14).

After downloading, you can transfer the content to your Studio One computer using a USB drive.

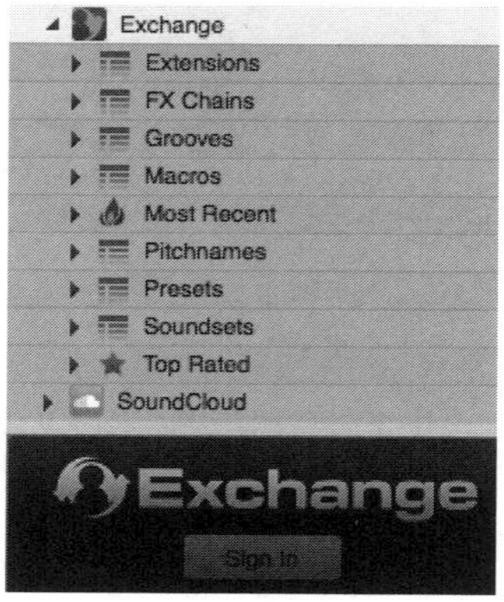

Figure 1-14

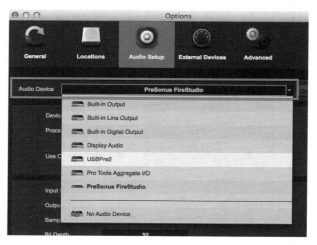

Figure 1-13

Audio Interface Setup

There are two parts to setting up your audio interface: selecting the audio device and setting up the Song.

Audio Device

To select which audio device to use, go to the Audio Setup tab in the Options dialog box (Cmd + Comma / Ctrl + Comma). From the audio device list, select the correct device. This is a global setting that affects all Songs and Projects.

Windows users can select any available ASIO device. Mac users can use any available Core Audio device.

Figure 1-15

Song Setup

The second part of setting up an audio interface takes place in the Song Setup dialog box of each Song (Song > Song Setup > Audio I/O Setup). I/O routing is done on a Song-by-Song basis. However, you can save any configuration as the default so that you won't need to do this every time you start a new Song.

The I/O routing matrix in Song Setup lets you map software inputs and outputs to hardware on the interface.

In addition, you can give your I/O friendly names like SM7, Rhodes, Nora, Auratones—whatever makes sense to you.

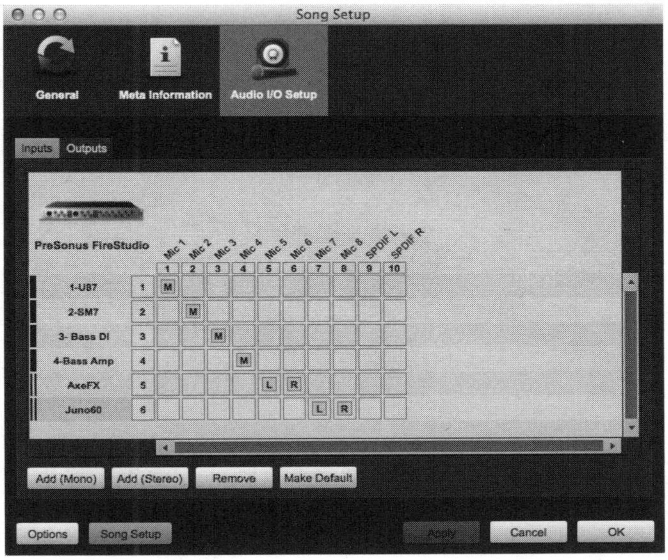

Mapping Inputs

Select the Inputs tab in Audio I/O Setup. Hardware inputs are listed along the top of the grid. Software inputs are listed along the left side. You can add software inputs using the buttons below the grid as mono or stereo inputs. You can remove an input by first selecting one, then clicking on Remove.

To assign hardware to the software inputs, just click on the box in the grid under the input to assign. This creates a route between hardware and software. If you move the Song to a different computer, just come back to this screen and make new hardware assignments.

Double-click on any of the software input names to edit them. Use this method to rename inputs with friendly names to identify inputs with friendly names.

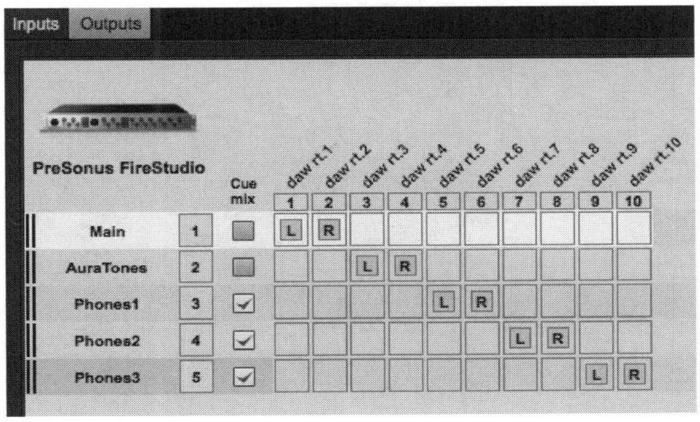

Mapping Outputs

Select the Outputs tab in Audio I/O Setup. Set up the outputs the same way you did for inputs. For each software output you assign, a new output channel will be added to the mixer. If you plan to use outputs as cue mixes, click on the Cue option in that row.

The Cue option has special meaning when used with PreSonus interfaces. I will go over that in more detail in the section on zero-latency monitoring.

Figure 1-16

Figure 1-17

Studio One Terminology

Studio One has specific terminology for key concepts, some of which deviates from terminology used with other DAWs.

Songs

A Song is called a "project" in most other systems. As you might expect, a Song contains the tracks and mix setup for a song. The main recording, editing, and mixing view is called the Song page. You will use the Song page for recording, editing, applying effects, using virtual instruments, and mixing.

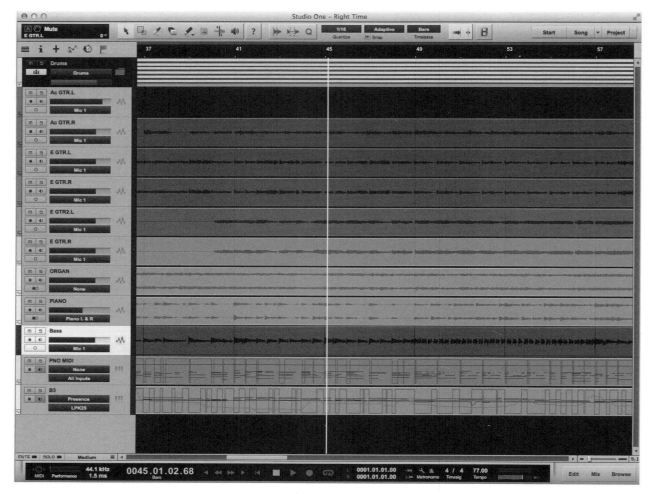

Figure 1-18

Projects

A Project is essentially a collection of Songs that make up an album. It organizes the Songs into tracks. The main page that holds the Track List and Timeline is called the Project page. You will use the Project page to create CD images, DDP files, and digital releases.

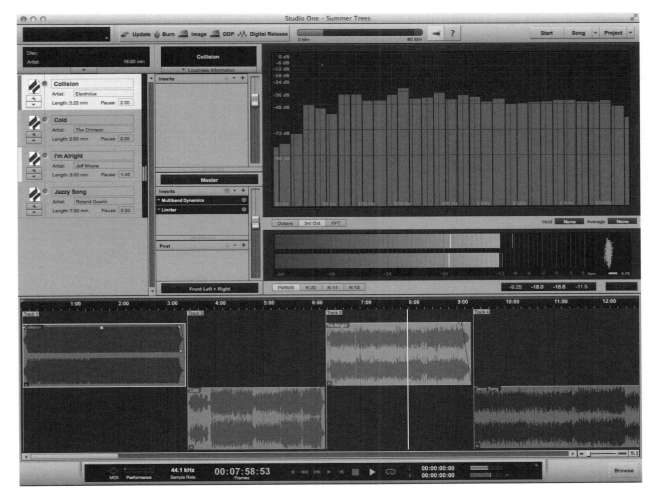

Figure 1-19

Events

In most DAW software a snippet of audio or instrument notes on the Timeline is called a "clip." Until recently Pro Tools users called this a "region." Logic still calls this concept a "region." However, in Studio One a snippet of audio or instrument Notes on the Timeline is called an Event. There are three types of Events: Audio Events, Audio Parts, and Instrument Parts.

Figure 1-20

An Audio Event contains a single audio waveform. An Audio Part contains audio that's been separated into slices. An Instrument Part contains Note data. Audio Events and Audio Parts are found on Audio Tracks. Instrument Parts are found only on Instrument Tracks. I will explain the types of Events more fully later in this book.

MIDI

Technically, Studio One doesn't use MIDI to record and edit Instrument Part performances. It uses a higher-resolution method to record and define virtual instrument tracks. In keeping with this idea, Studio One documentation avoids calling anything MIDI except in reference to connecting hardware MIDI ports. In Studio One there are Instrument Tracks (MIDI tracks), which contain Instrument Parts (a type of Event), which contain Notes (like a MIDI event).

Keyboard Shortcuts

Most actions in Studio One can be assigned to keyboard shortcuts. The most common commands are preassigned and will appear next to menu items or as tooltips when you point at onscreen controls. You can view or print a complete list of shortcuts by going to Help > Keyboard Shortcuts. This will open an HTML file of all assigned shortcuts for your system. Additionally, at the end of each chapter of this book I have compiled a list of relevant keyboard shortcuts.

You can completely customize keyboard shortcut assignments under Studio One > Keyboard Shortcuts. This takes you to the Keyboard Shortcuts tab of the Options dialog box. Here you can search for actions, make shortcut assignments, create your own keyboard assignments, and load maps that make Studio One emulate Pro Tools, Cubase, or Logic.

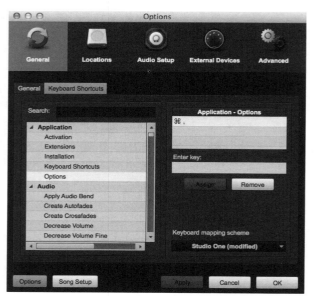

Figure 1-21

Getting Help

Certainly this book is a great resource for learning Studio One features. As you learn, you will certainly want to take advantage of the following additional learning opportunities:

Figure 1-22

Reference Manual. The Studio One reference manual is a clear, concise reference to all commands and features of Studio One. It is a searchable PDF and can be accessed from Studio One > Help > Contents.

Info View. The Question Mark icon on the Toolbar activates Info view. Info view shows keyboard modifiers for editing using the mouse tools. It is an essential aid when getting started with Studio One.

PreSonus Forum. The PreSonus forum (Figure 1-23) is particularly friendly and knowledgeable. You can search the forum, post questions, bring up issues, or make feature requests. Passionate users along with PreSonus staff, developers, and lowly authors often visit the forum to discuss features, new releases, and creative ways to use Studio One.

Studio One Website. PreSonus maintains a website specifically for Studio One (Figure 1-24). This site has numerous tutorial videos, a knowledge base, access to technical support, and information about live-stream demos.

PreSonuSphere. PreSonus also hosts PreSonuSphere, the annual users group meeting held in Baton Rouge, Louisiana. PreSonuSphere is a fantastic opportunity to meet other users and watch live presentations on Studio One features. You might even meet me there!

Figure 1-23

Layout and Navigation

You will likely find the Studio One screen layout to be logical and easy to grasp, if not familiar. Likewise, basic navigation is straightforward but flexible.

Figure 1-24

Song Page Screen Layout

The Studio One Song page has a straightforward layout that is organized into several key sections:

Arrange View. Arrange view is equivalent to what is called Track view or Edit view in other DAWs. Audio Events and Instrument Parts have separate track types. Audio can be edited directly in Arrange view. Instrument Parts can be split, stretched, and trimmed in Arrange view, but editing of individual Notes must be done in the Music Editor. In other words, there is no inline MIDI editor.

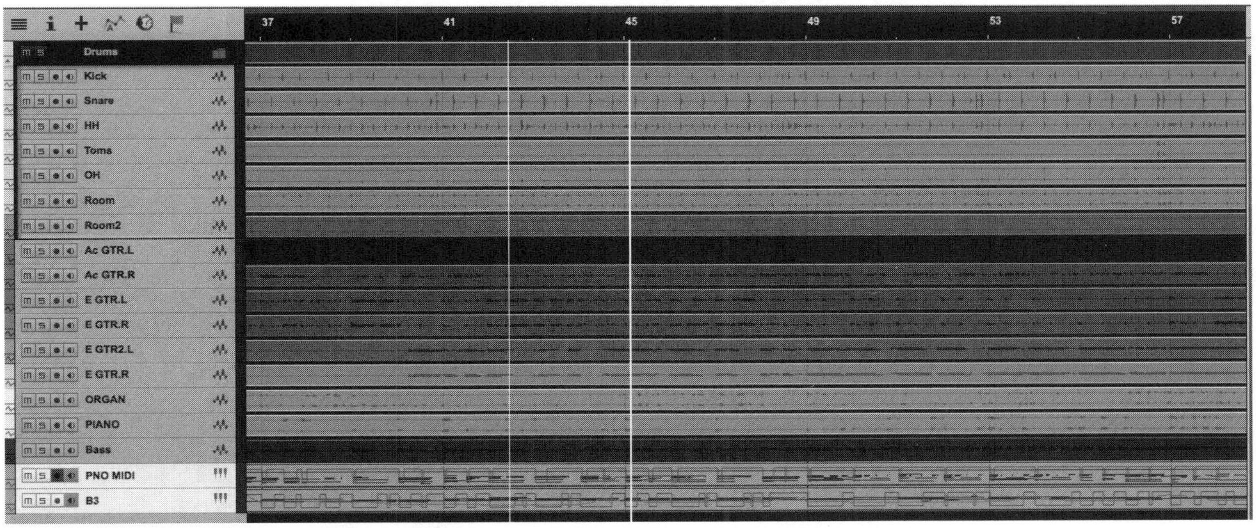

Figure 1-25

Toolbar. The Toolbar contains mouse tools for edit, snap, and quantize settings, Control Link setup, and cursor control.

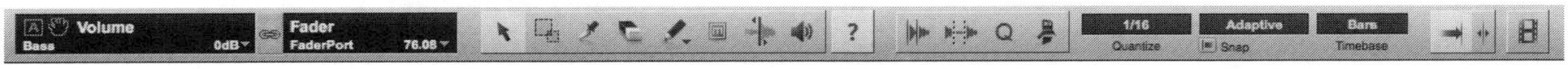

Figure 1-26

Inspector. The Inspector view contains essential settings to adjust the properties of the selected Track and Event. This view also gives you access to the powerful Event FX feature.

Figure 1-27   Figure 1-28

Browser. The Browser is actually several browsers in one. It allows access to your file system, effects, instruments, and sounds, as well as the media pool for the current Song. Drag-and-drop is the key concept here. Almost anything can be dragged from the Browser and dropped on your project.

Console View. The Console view is a virtual mixing console. It gives you a full overview of your mix, along with access to inputs, outputs, and buses. It can be docked or detached so you can move it to your second monitor, and expanded to full screen.

Figure 1-29

Editor. The Editor works as a detail view for the currently selected track. For Audio Parts, it allows access to individual slices. The Editor docks at the bottom of the main window but can be detached and displayed on a second monitor.

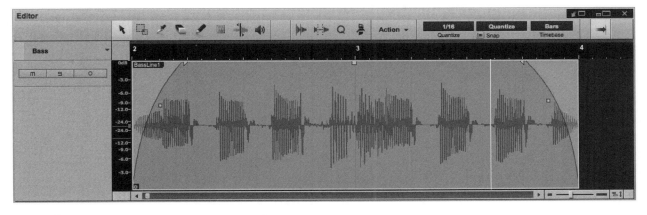

Figure 1-30

Music Editor. When you double-click on an Instrument Part, the editor becomes a Music Editor, allowing detailed editing of Note data. Other systems would call this view a piano-roll view, PRV, or MIDI editor.

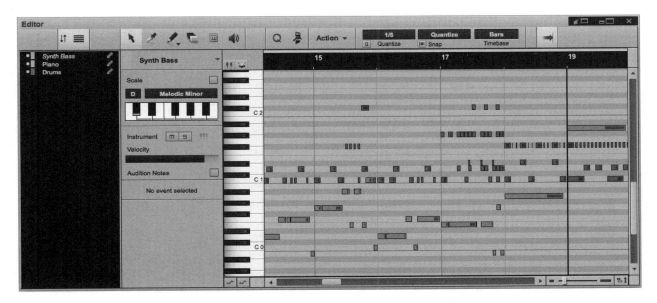

Figure 1-31

Transport Bar. The play, stop, record, loop, metronome, and punch-in controls are located on the Transport bar at the bottom edge of the program. It is not detachable, movable or floating, but on high-resolution monitors you can use the Wrench icon (far right) to position it flush left, flush right, or centered. If your screen doesn't have enough resolution, the wrench will not appear.

Figure 1-32

Transport Controls

Although standard transport controls are available on the Transport bar, you will probably want to use keyboard shortcuts instead.

The default keyboard assignments are as follows:

- Play/Stop: Spacebar
- Return to Zero: Comma
- Forward: Numpad +
- Rewind: Numpad −

Note that the Spacebar will toggle play and stop, but you can decide if you want the playback cursor to pause right where you stopped or return to where playback started (Options > Return to Start on Stop).

Like most every action in Studio One, the Transport keyboard shortcuts can be completely reassigned in Options.

> **Tip:** There are numerous actions related to Transport controls that are available but not assigned to the keyboard. To see what's available, search for "Transport" on the keyboard shortcut assignment dialog box (Studio One > Keyboard Shortcuts).

Zooming

To zoom in and zoom out horizontally, drag up and down on the Tmeline ruler. This will be familiar to Live and Cubase users.

The following are the essential keyboard shortcuts for zooming:

- Zoom In: E
- Zoom Out: W
- Zoom In Vertical: Shift + E
- Zoom Out Vertical: Shift + W

If you are used to Pro Tools, you might want to reassign zooming to "R" and "T" to avoid confusion. There are many other zoom actions available under View > Zoom.

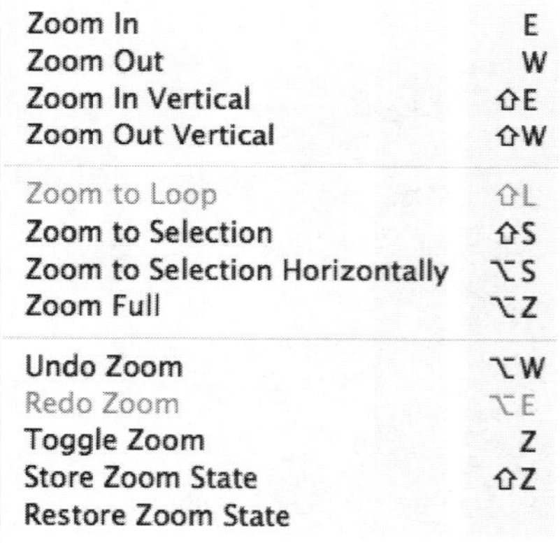

Zoom In	E
Zoom Out	W
Zoom In Vertical	⇧E
Zoom Out Vertical	⇧W
Zoom to Loop	⇧L
Zoom to Selection	⇧S
Zoom to Selection Horizontally	⌥S
Zoom Full	⌥Z
Undo Zoom	⌥W
Redo Zoom	⌥E
Toggle Zoom	Z
Store Zoom State	⇧Z
Restore Zoom State	

Figure 1-33

> **Tip:** I often like to zoom in horizontally to focus on Events I am editing. To do this, select the event and press P to set the loop over the selection. Then, press Shift + L to zoom to the loop.

Undo

Studio One maintains an undo history of most actions. Pressing Cmd + Z / Ctrl + Z undoes the most recent action. You can use the History dialog box to access a complete undo history for the current session (Edit > History).

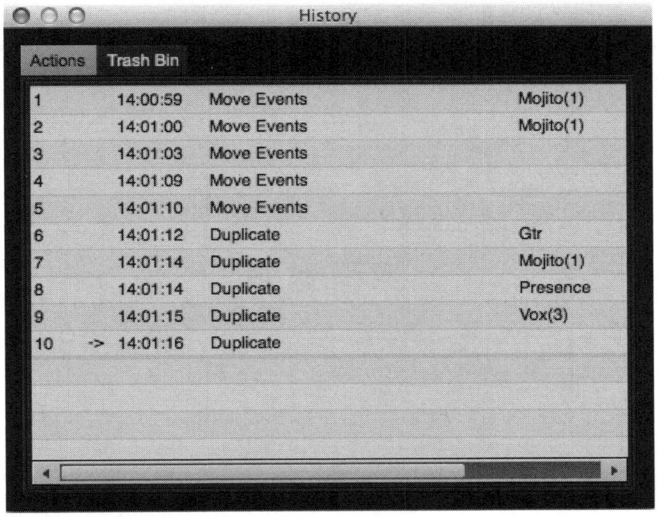

Figure 1-34

The History dialog box has a tab for the Trash bin. Use this to restore any effects or instruments you may have deleted from the Song. You can also access the Trash bin from the Console view using the Trash button on the far left.

Chapter 2
SONGS

In this chapter I will take a look at how to create and manage Songs and how to import existing material into a Song. A Song in Studio One is essentially a project. It is a set of folders and files that contain the media and mix of a song. In many other digital audio workstations (DAWs) this concept is called a "project" or "session." In Studio One it is simply called a Song. All recording, editing, and mixing is done in the Song page.

Creating Songs

To create a new Song, launch the New Song dialog box from the Start page. You can also get to the New Song dialog box from the menu at any time (File > New Song). Here you can enter the song title, path to the Song folder, and audio properties. You can also choose a template for the Song from on the left side.

Figure 2-1

Where Are Songs Stored?

Each Song is stored in its own folder under the Studio One Songs folder. The song title is the name of the folder for that Song. By default, Song folders will be created in the User Data folder. By default the user data folder will be located in your Documents folder and named Studio One.

You can change the name and location of the User Data folder in the Locations tab of the Options dialog box. When you create a new Song, you can override the default location and store Songs anywhere you like on your file system.

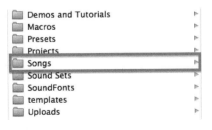

Figure 2-2

Figure 2-3

The actual Song file is the song title with a .song extension. You can browse through a song file using the Studio One Browser. To do this, navigate to the Song file, right-click, and select Show Package Contents. This allows you to expand the Song file to view presets, channels, performances, and other Song elements. You can even drag these elements into other Songs.

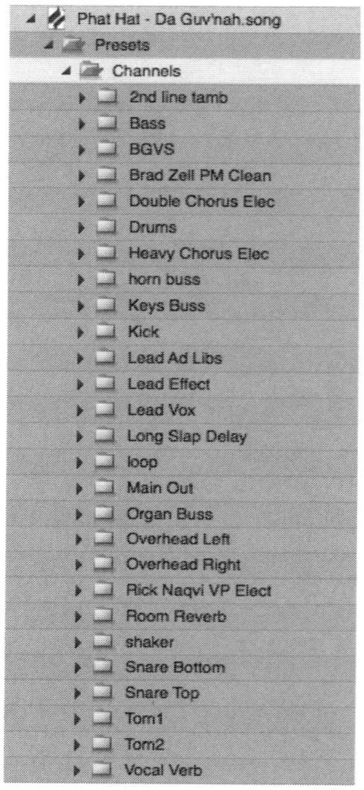

Backing Up

To back up a Song, copy the entire Song folder to an external drive or system. A Song folder may contain several subfolders including bounces, cache, history, stems, master, media, and mixdown.

Note that if you drag samples, loops, or sounds into a Song, they won't be automatically copied to the Song folder. To make sure you are backing up everything, select Song > Copy External Files before making a backup. You can also make a backup by right-clicking in the Browser Pool tab and selecting it from the context menu. There is an important setting in the Options dialog box related to this.

I advise you to set this option so that the external files will be copied to the Song as you exit. This way the Song folder will always contain everything needed to back up or move the Songs to a different computer.

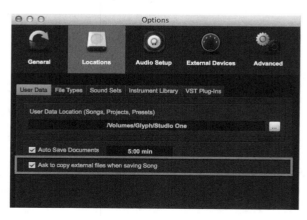

Figure 2-4

Saving

Cmd + S / Ctrl + S saves the current Song in Studio One. If you try to close the Song before saving, Studio One will ask if you wish to save it. Oftentimes, you will add a loop or recording to a Song, only to find that it is not the right fit. When this

Figure 2-5

happens, you can unlink the unused media from the Song using Song > Remove Unused Files. You can also do this from the Browser Pool tab by right-clicking on the media list.

Note: This only removes references to unused files so you don't see them in the pool—it does not delete any media from the Song folder. To actually clear out unused files, copy the Song to a new folder (File > Save to New Folder), and then delete the old folder. Don't delete it right away, however! Make sure the new copy of the Song loads and works properly first.

| Refresh |
| Locate Missing Files... |
| Remove Unused Files |
| Copy External Files... |
| Show Media Folder in Finder |

Figure 2-6

Revision History

At any point you can save a snapshot of a Song by choosing File > Save New Version. Here is where you to write any notes that will help you remember the significance of this version. You can return to this version at any time by choosing File > Restore Version.

Figure 2-7

> **Tip:** Save a new version before making major edits or deletions. I also save versions before and after tracking sessions. Adding notes like "before comping lead vocal" or "after tracking lead guitar" will really help you understand the reason for each version.

Note: The revision history is lost when saving to a new folder (File > Save to New Folder).

Importing Audio

To import audio, drag an audio file into the Arrange view. If you drop it on the background, Studio One will automatically create a track and an Audio Event. If you drop the file on an existing track, Studio One will convert it to an Audio Event. You can drag files from the Browser or from your file system. Studio One supports a wide variety of audio file types.

Studio One will attempt to stretch imported audio files to match the song tempo depending on the track settings. You can override this in the New Song dialog box.

Figure 2-8

For existing Songs, you can change set this in Song Setup area on the General tab.

Figure 2-9

This setting only affects files imported after making the change. If you don't want imported audio to be stretched, you can change the Tempo property for the track to Don't Follow in the Inspector.

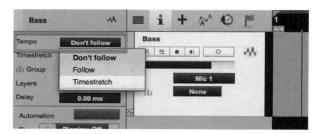

Figure 2-10

Snap Settings

The Quantize, Snap, and Timebase properties on the Toolbar help you work with the timing of events on the tracks in Arrange view. They do this by establishing the snap grid, which is a grid laid across the tracks representing the Song's time signature and quantize setting. The Quantize setting allows you to select musical divisions like eighth or quarter notes to define the grid. As you move events they can snap to the grid if you have Snap turned on.

Figure 2-11

With the snap mode set to Adaptive, the grid increments represent different rhythmic values, depending on the zoom level. As you zoom in, the rhythmic values get smaller, so the increments will go from representing entire measures to representing quarter notes to representing eighth notes and so on. The purpose of this grid and these functions is to allow you to accurately align events to musical time while editing.

Quantize

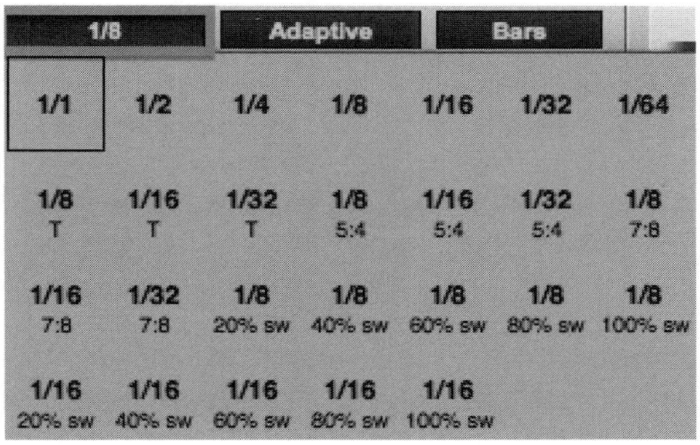

The Quantize value defines the snap grid in standard musical terms along with the time signature. For example, if you have Quantize set to eighths and the time signature set to 4/4, then the snap grid will be set with eight equal divisions per bar.

Figure 2-12

This setting does not actually do any quantizing on its own; it just establishes the grid. To actually adjust timing to the grid, you can use a variety of tools in Studio One including Snap, the Quantize panel, and Audio Bend. For both Audio and Instrument Tracks the simplest way to quantize is to set the Quantize parameter here and then hit Q. We will cover Quantize and Audio Bend in detail in a later section of this book.

Snap On/Off

Toggle Snap on and off using the Snap button or the keyboard shortcut N. In the Arrange view, snap makes it easy to align events to the grid. You can temporarily override snap by holding down the Shift key as you drag events.

Figure 2-13

As I just explained, the actual grid is defined by the quantize value. In Studio One, you can imagine the grid to be magnetic. With Snap on, events are attracted to the grid increments. If you get the beginning of an event close enough to the grid, it snaps in place. This is helpful when moving individual beats around in a drum part or when moving full Song sections around.

Snap Modes

Use the Snap property list to select from one of the four snap modes:

Adaptive. This will snap to the grid defined in the quantize setting. Depending on the zoom level, you can locate events off the grid as well. This is the most common setting for music production. I leave the snap mode set to Adaptive at least 90% of the time.

Bar. This mode is a shortcut to allow snapping by measure. It is the same as setting the mode to Adaptive with Quantize at 1/1.

Quantize. When Timebase is set to Bars, this is the same thing as Adaptive. When Timebase is set to Seconds, this mode will snap to the nearest second.

Figure 2-14

Frames. This allows snapping by Frames for film or video work. It is the same thing as setting the mode to Adaptive and the Timebase to Frames.

Snap Behaviors

Snap also has four behaviors that are grouped at the bottom of the Snap properties list:

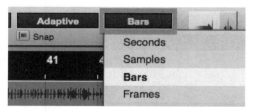

Figure 2-15

Snap to Cursor and Loop. This option makes the loop in and out points and the cursor magnetic, as if they were part of the grid.

Snap to Events. This makes events snap to other events on the same or other tracks. This behavior makes it easy to organize events end to end.

Snap to Grid. This causes magnetic objects to snap to the grid defined in the Quantize property list. This is the default, and you need to have this option set for normal snapping to work.

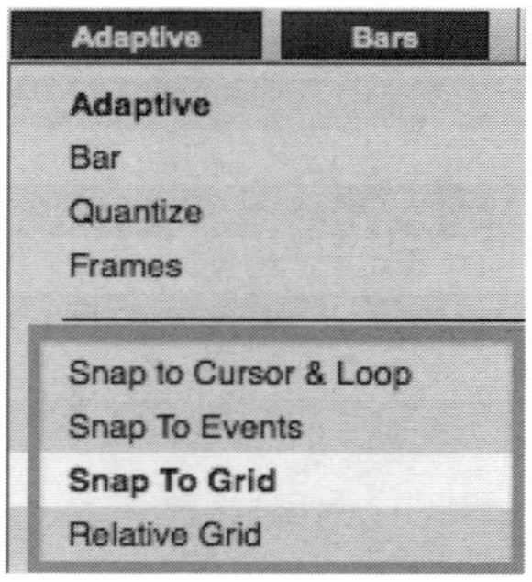

Relative Grid. This is a modifier to Snap to Grid. This keeps track of where an event was positioned relative to the grid at the start of a drag-move operation and uses that for the destination position. For example, if you drag an event that begins a moment before the downbeat, you can position it correctly related to the destination downbeat. This is very similar to Relative Grid mode in Pro Tools.

Most music production editing is done with the snap mode set to Adaptive and with Snap to Grid as the only behavior enabled.

Timebase

The Timebase property sets the units of the snap grid and has several options:

Figure 2-16

Seconds. With Timebase set to Seconds, the grid appears as hours, minutes, and seconds. The finest grid increment is 10 ms. This is useful for music production in which the music is played freely without a click or grid. It is also useful for voice-over, video, and film work. The Quantize property is ignored in this mode.

Samples. This value sets the grid to individual samples. I use this timebase for fixing glitches.

Bars. This sets the grid to musical divisions set by the Quantize property and time signature. This is the typical setting for music production.

Frames. Sets the grid to hours, minutes, seconds, and frames for film or video work. It is very similar to the Seconds setting, except that frames are used instead of fractional seconds. The Quantize property is ignored in this mode. The frame rate is set in the Song > Song Setup > General dialog box.

Chapter 3
TRACKS

In this chapter I demystify the various kinds of tracks in the Studio One Song page. I will get started by explaining the special Marker Track and Tempo Track. Then I will get into detail about Audio Tracks and Instrument Tracks, and touch on Automation Tracks.

Marker Track

Click on the Flag icon at the top of the Track header area to show or hide the Marker Track. Markers are on their own track, just below the Timeline ruler, to indicate important points in a song. Create a marker by placing the cursor in the desired location and pressing the Y key. You can also create a named marker by pressing Shift + Y. This is great for indicating the beginnings of song sections.

Figure 3-1

You can drag markers left and right in the Marker Track or delete them by hitting Delete on your keyboard. Right-clicking on a marker exposes properties and actions. Here you can edit the name, cut, copy, or delete.

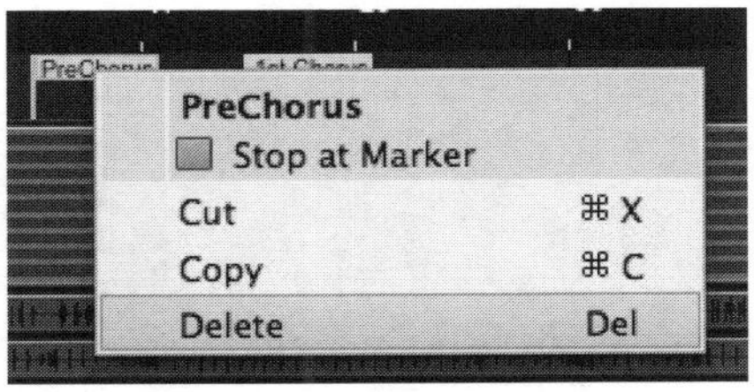

Right-clicking on a marker also reveals the Stop at Marker option. With this set, playback will stop at the marker. This is useful when you want to automatically stop playback or recording at a certain point in the song. I often use this option while tracking alone in order to avoid the need to grab for the keyboard or mouse after a take.

Figure 3-2

Figure 3-3

Note: The Marker Track contains special blue start and end markers that identify the song start and end. These mark what part of the Song to use for exporting mixes or stems. These can be moved and renamed like other markers but cannot be deleted.

Navigating with Markers

If you use markers for your song sections, you can go to the next marker by pressing Shift + N and go to the previous marker by pressing Shift + B. If you have an extended keyboard, you can use numbers 3 through 9 on the numeric keypad for direct access to the first seven markers.

Remember that these assignments are just the defaults. If you use markers a lot, you might want to assign them directly to numbers 1 through 9 on the Numpad.

Tempo Track

Studio One has a special Tempo Track used to mark tempo changes anywhere in a Song. In this section I will explain how to set the tempo for both fixed- and variable-tempo Songs.

Setting a Single Fixed Tempo

If your song has one fixed tempo, you can set the tempo on the Transport bar. Click on the tempo value and type in the new tempo or, alternatively, drag left or right to change the tempo.

You can also tap with mouse-clicks on the word "tempo" just below the value to set it based on the beats per minute (bpm) of your clicks. I usually use this trick only when the Song is still

Figure 3-4

empty. Otherwise, if the Song has much data in it Studio One will start working really hard trying to stretch everything to match your varying taps.

Setting Tempo Changes

If the tempo varies during the Song, you can define the tempo changes in the Tempo Track. To do this, open the Tempo Track by clicking on the clock icon above the Track header area.

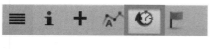

Figure 3-5

Position the cursor where you would like a tempo change to occur and click on the Plus icon on the Tempo Track header to insert the tempo change. Then, update the tempo value on the Tempo Track header or on the Transport bar.

Figure 3-6

Alternatively, drag up and down on the top edge of a Tempo region to change the tempo. For more detailed editing of tempo maps, you can hold down Cmd / Ctrl while dragging a tempo change. This will allow you to stretch the tempo horizontally. Holding down Shift as you drag will give you finer control over tempo adjustment.

You can also move the location of a tempo change by dragging it along the Timeline. Using these tools you can adjust the tempo or create tempo maps.

Time Signature

A Song's time signature is set in the Transport bar by clicking on and selecting the desired values. To insert a time signature change within the Song, right-click on the Timeline ruler and select Insert Timesignature. A dialog box will appear where you can specify the time signature. After you do this, a time signature marker will appear on the Timeline. You can drag to move it, or right-click to edit or remove it.

Figure 3-7

About Tracks

Studio One supports Audio and Instrument Tracks in the Arrange view. Both share many common features, but for now I will focus on Audio Tracks.

Creating Tracks

You can create one or more tracks from the Add Tracks dialog box. This can be accessed by pressing the keyboard shortcut T. It can also be accessed through the menu (Track > Add Tracks) or with the Plus icon above the Track header area.

Figure 3-8

The Add Tracks dialog box allows you to name the track, select how many tracks to add, select the format of the track, load a track preset, and select the track color. To quickly add a single track, right-click in some blank space in the Track header column and choose the track type from the list.

To save time, I often just duplicate an existing track and rename it. Right-click on an existing track and choose Duplicate Track. This works great if you want a new track with the same basic setup.

Track Size

You can select the vertical size for all tracks at the bottom of the Track header column. Here, you can choose from size presets like large, medium, and small, or use the slider to adjust the size freely.

Figure 3-9

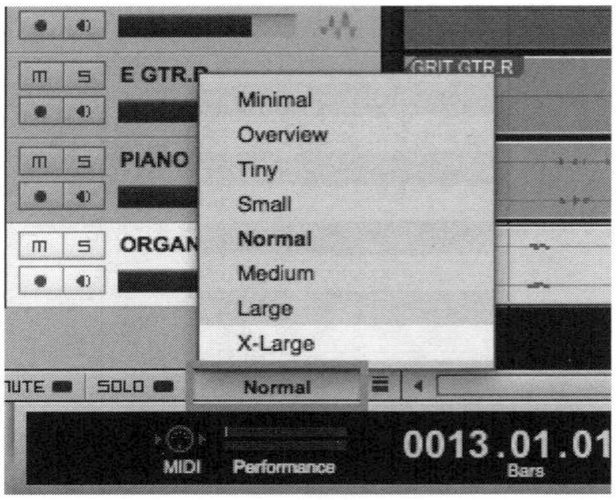

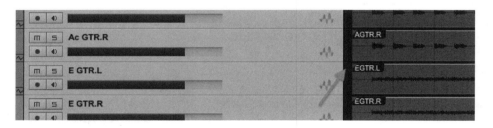

Figure 3-10

Adjust the vertical size of one or more selected tracks by grabbing the bottom edge of a track and dragging it up or down. If you have long track names that are getting truncated, you can also adjust their width by grabbing the right edge of any Track header and dragging it outward.

Figure 3-11

Track Types

There are five kinds of tracks that can be selected with the Format property in the Add Tracks dialog box:

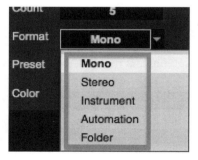

Figure 3-12

Mono Audio Track. Mono Audio Tracks allow recording and editing of Audio Events. Mono tracks have single input assignment and a mono output. If you record to a mono track, the resulting Audio Events will be mono.

Stereo Audio Track. Stereo Audio Tracks can have stereo or mono input assignments. They always have stereo output. When you record to a stereo track, the resulting Audio Events will be stereo. Note that you can easily switch the track mode from mono to stereo using the Channel Mode button. Channel Mode buttons are available on each track and in the Inspector.

Instrument Track. Instrument Tracks are essentially MIDI tracks. An Instrument Track is typically routed to a virtual instrument in the Console. The Instrument Track itself doesn't contain a virtual instrument, only Instrument Parts (essentially MIDI data). You can also route an Instrument Track to external MIDI sound devices.

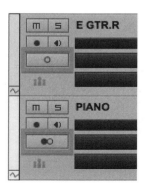

Figure 3-13

Automation Track. Automation for any parameter can exist as part of an Audio or Instrument Track or as a separate track. The easiest way to create an Automation Track is to grab any control onscreen and drag the Hand icon from Control Link to the Arrange view.

Figure 3-14

Folder Track. Folder Tracks are containers for any of the other track types. They are great organizational and workflow tools.

Audio Track Controls

Audio and Instrument Tracks have slightly different track controls. I will go over the details of Instrument Tracks a bit later, but for now let's focus on Audio Tracks. If some of these controls are not visible, increase the track height to reveal them.

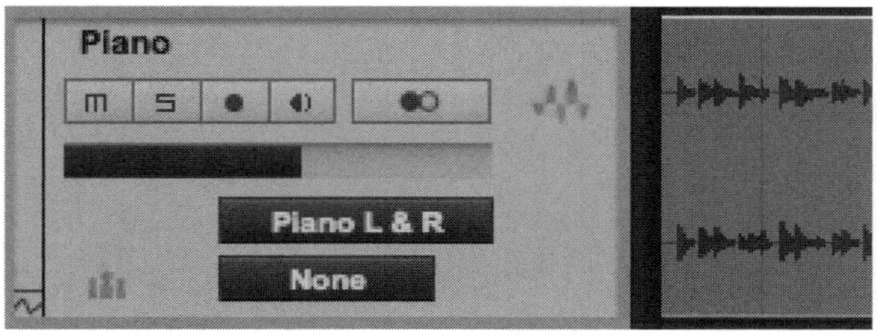

Figure 3-15

Each Audio Track contains these common controls:

Mute. Pressing the M key toggles the Mute feature on and off for the selected track or tracks, as does the M button on each Track header. There is also a master Mute button at the bottom of the Track header column to clear or toggle the current mute selections.

Solo. Pressing S toggles Solo on and off. This enables a track to play back while all other tracks are muted. You can solo multiple tracks simultaneously by soloing each of them. There is also a master Solo button at the bottom of the Track header column to clear or toggle the solo selections. If you solo a grouped track, all tracks in the Group will be soloed.

Track Name. Double-click on the track name to edit it. Note: Studio One uses the track name as the basis for event names during recording and bouncing.

Record Enable. This feature arms a track for recording. The keyboard shortcut R does the same thing. Arming a track is prerequisite to recording using the Record button in the Transport.

Input Monitor. This option allows monitoring live sound through the input and associated console channel. Typically, this monitoring path will include a delay of several milliseconds, depending on hardware buffer settings. Use the keyboard shortcut U or the Speaker icon in the Track header to enable or disable input monitoring.

Figure 3-16

Volume. The Track Volume slider is on the Track header for convenience. The same control is available in the Inspector and on the Console.

Track Icon. The Wave icon indicates that this is an Audio Track.

Figure 3-17

Input Selection. Click on the parameter and select any available software input or open Audio I/O Setup.

Group Assignment. Click on the parameter to assign the track to any available group. To clear the group assignment, set this parameter to "none."

Figure 3-18

Instrument Track Controls

Instrument Tracks have similar controls to Audio Tracks. Since Instrument Tracks contain only Note data, they point to a virtual instrument as sound source. As a result the track parameters are a bit different.

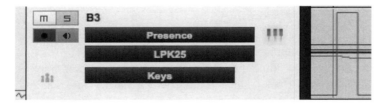

Figure 3-19

Mute. Mute is a toggle of either the Mute button or the M key on the keyboard. As with Audio Tracks, Mute keeps a track from playing back. For Instrument Tracks, Mute silences the data stream sent to the virtual instrument, but doesn't take it offline.

Solo. Toggle Solo with S or the Solo button. Solo allows you to quickly isolate a single track or a few tracks to play back. Click on Solo on a track, and it will play back with the other tracks muted. If you click on Solo on additional tracks, you will hear them during playback as well. Note that there is a master Solo button at the bottom of the Track header column to clear or toggle the Solo selections.

Track Name. Double-click on the track name to edit it. Note that Studio One uses the track name as the basis for event names during recording and bouncing.

Record Enable. Record-enable arms a track for recording. To record an Instrument Track requires some sort of controller—typically a keyboard.

Input Monitor. The Speaker icon or the U key on the keyboard enables input monitoring. This allows monitoring live sound through the input and associated console channel. Note that his must be on for Instrument Tracks. Otherwise, you won't hear playback or be able to play from a controller.

Volume. The Track Volume slider is on the Track header for convenience. The same control is available in the Inspector and on the Console. This controls the volume of the associated virtual instrument.

Track Icon. This icon indicates that this is an Instrument Track. Click on the icon to show the user interface for the associated virtual instrument.

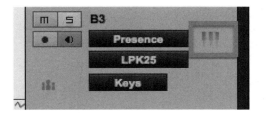

Figure 3-20

Output Selection. Click on the parameter and select any available virtual instrument or MIDI output.

Group Assignment. Click on the parameter to assign the track to any available group. To clear the group assignment, set this parameter to "none."

Track Layers

Each track can have multiple layers of audio data. Only one layer per track will be active (audible) at a time. This same concept exists in many other DAWs by the same name. Pro Tools users refer to layers as "playlists."

It is easy to loop record and build composite tracks using layers. I will cover those in detail later on, but for now I want to go over the basic tools for working with layers.

Actions to add, duplicate, rename, and remove layers can be found on the menu Track > Layers. By default these are not mapped to the keyboard. Personally, since I commonly add layers during tracking, I assign Add Layer to the Backslash key, or "\".

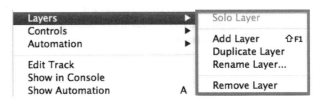

Figure 3-21

The same commands are also available by right-clicking on the header for a track under Layers and by clicking on the Layers property in the Inspector. If a track has more than one layer, you can choose to see all the layers in separate lanes. That option is available near the top of the right-click menu for the track.

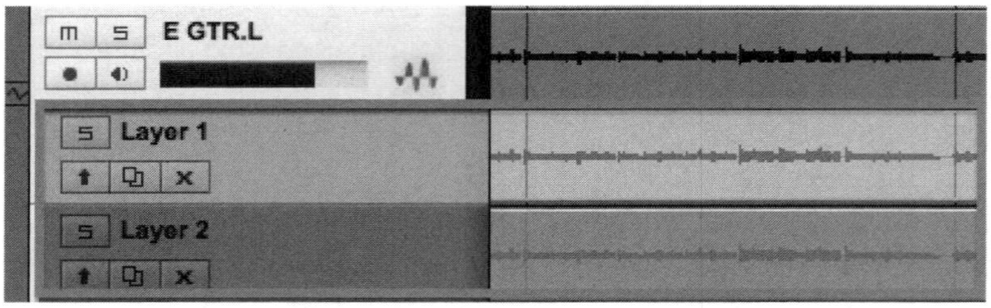

Figure 3-22

Figure 3-23

When the layers are expanded, each layer has its own Track header controls that let you solo, activate, duplicate, or remove it. Activate makes this layer the active layer. This is the same as selecting the layer from the Layer property in the Inspector.

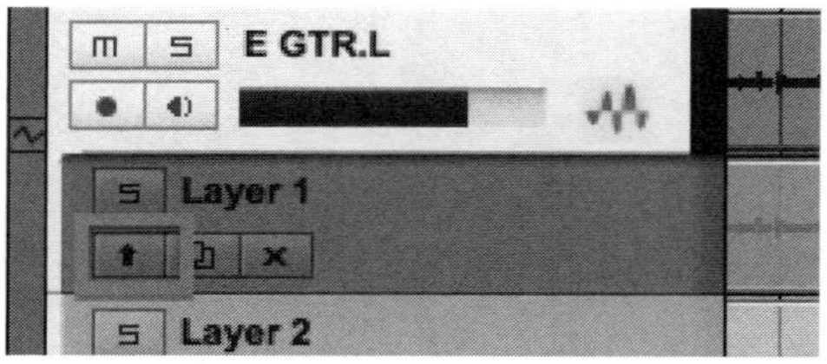

Figure 3-24

Track Groups

Track groups are used to organize several tracks into a single Group. These are essential when editing multitrack drums because they help keep parts from going out of phase while editing or using Audio Bend. Groups are also very helpful for organizing similar tracks such as harmony vocal tracks.

When an Audio Track is grouped, the corresponding console channel is also grouped. When an Instrument Track is grouped, the associated virtual Instrument Channels in the Console are also grouped.

Here are the essential commands for working with groups in Studio One:

Group Selected Tracks. Group any selection of tracks by pressing Cmd + G / Ctrl + G or by making your choice from the right-click menu. This groups tracks for editing and mixing in the Arrange view and the Console.

Figure 3-25

Group Override. You can temporarily override a group by holding Opt / Alt while moving the Track Volume or other controls.

Adding a Track to a Group. You can add a track to any existing track group with the Group property in the Inspector.

Figure 3-26

Removing a Track from a Group. Remove a track from a group by setting the Group property in the Track header to "none."

Dissolving a Group. Dissolve a Group entirely by choosing Shift + Cmd + G / Shift + Ctrl + G or by using the right-click menu.

Folder Tracks

Folder Tracks allow you to keep Songs with high track counts organized, by collapsing several tracks into the space of one. They have simple features to create groups, create buses, or add effects to the tracks in the folder.

Creating Folder Tracks

Select the tracks you want to put into a folder, then select Pack Folder from the right-click menu. You can also right-click on the empty area in the Track header column and select Add Folder Track. This will add a new empty Folder Track. Then add tracks to the Folder Track by dragging them in.

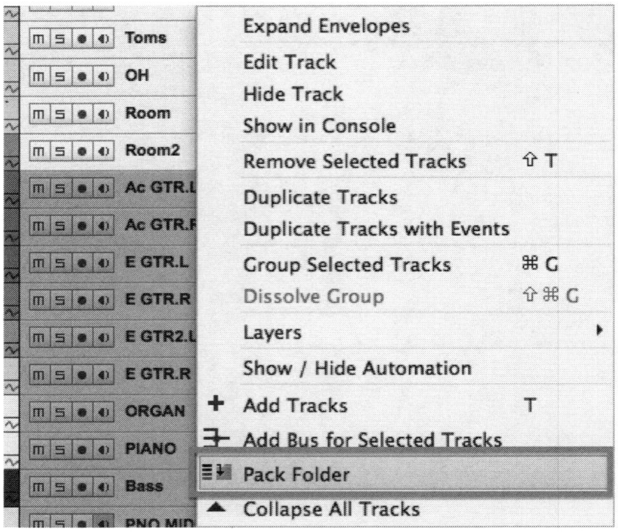

m s • ◄) Toms	Expand Envelopes
m s • ◄) OH	Edit Track
m s • ◄) Room	Hide Track
m s • ◄) Room2	Show in Console
m s • ◄) Ac GTR.L	Remove Selected Tracks ⇧ T
m s • ◄) Ac GTR.R	Duplicate Tracks
m s • ◄) E GTR.L	Duplicate Tracks with Events
m s • ◄) E GTR.R	Group Selected Tracks ⌘ G
m s • ◄) E GTR2.L	Dissolve Group ⇧⌘ G
m s • ◄) E GTR.R	Layers ▸
m s • ◄) ORGAN	Show / Hide Automation
m s • ◄) PIANO	✚ Add Tracks T
m s • ◄) Bass	⫪ Add Bus for Selected Tracks
m s • ◄) PNO MID	▤Ɱ Pack Folder
	▲ Collapse All Tracks

Figure 3-27

Folder Track Properties

Folder Tracks have similar properties to ordinary tracks, except most properties apply to every track in the folder. The color and track name are specific to the Folder Track itself.

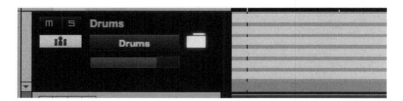

Figure 3-28

Mute (M). Mute all tracks in the folder.
Solo (S). Solo all the tracks in the folder.
Name. Double-click on the folder name to edit it.
Group. Instantly create a group for mixing and editing all the tracks in the folder. I love this feature!

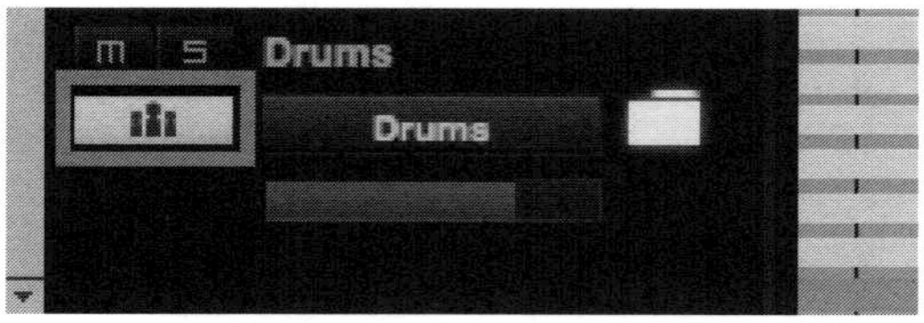

Figure 3-29

Bus Channels. Use this property to assign all tracks in the Folder Track to a Bus Channel (similar to "Aux Input" in Pro Tools). You can create a Bus Channel from the menu. The new Bus Channel will be automatically named after the Folder Track. This feature is a huge time-saver.

Figure 3-30

Icon. Folder Tracks are indicated with the Folder icon. Clicking on the icon will expand and collapse the folder, revealing or hiding its contents.

Figure 3-31

Volume. If you have assigned the Folder Track to a Bus Channel, the volume control allows you to tweak the bus mix right in the Arrange view.

Figure 3-32

Adding Effects to Folder Tracks

If you have assigned a Folder Track to a bus as described above, you can easily add effects to the folder. Simply drag any effect from the Browser and drop it on the folder. It will be assigned to the associated Bus Channel as an insert effect.

Resizing Folder Tracks

Folder Tracks can be resized just like other tracks by grabbing and dragging the lower or right edge of the header. As you increase the vertical size, you can see the outline of the Events contained in the folder.

Nesting Folder Tracks

You can set up folders within folders if you like. This is helpful for saving space. For example, if you have a drum folder, you may like to create a subfolder for all of your snare mics. Collapsing the top-level Folder Track will collapse all lower-level Folder Tracks.

Keep in mind that if you create a Bus Channel for a folder within a folder, it will automatically route to the Main Out—not the Bus Channel of the higher-level folder. In the example used in the last paragraph, this means that a Bus Channel created for the snare mics would not automatically route to the Bus Channel created for the drums. Routing can be changed manually in the Console view.

Track List

Open the Track List view by clicking on the four-line icon at the top of the Track header column.

Figure 3-33

You may want to assign a keyboard shortcut to this if you use it frequently. The Track List shows all the tracks in a very compact hierarchy with several columns, a set of filters at the bottom, and a useful preset system.

Track List Columns

The Track List has six columns of information and controls:

Figure 3-34

1. **Meter.** The meter is a tiny version of the track level meter. It helps you understand what tracks have activity from this view.

2. **Hide/Show Icon.** Click on this icon for any track to toggle it between being shown and hidden. You can also drag over this column to select or hide or show several tracks at a time.

3. **Icon.** The Track icon indicates the track type. Click on a track's icon to select the track. Drag from this icon to move the track up or down in the list.

4. **Color.** The small color bar is the track color. You can't set it from here, but it helps you relate the Track List to the tracks in the Arrange view.

5. **Track Name.** Click on the track name to expand the track to show more track details like automation and layers or to expand Folder Tracks. Clicking again will collapse that level.

6. **Group.** Group shows what Group the track is assigned to. If no Group is assigned, it will be blank.

Track List Filters

The filter section at the bottom edge of the Track List allows you to quickly hide or show tracks by type and to synchronize the Arrange view to the Console view.

Track Types. Click on any of these track types to instantly hide them from the Arrange view. From left to right the track types are Audio Tracks, Instrument Tracks, Folder Tracks, and Automation Tracks. When the button appears dark, that type of track is hidden.

Figure 3-35

Layers. Click on the Layers button to collapse the Layers view for any tracks with layers.

Figure 3-36

Envelopes. If you have expanded any of the tracks to show automation envelopes by clicking on the track name in the Track List, this button will allow you to show or hide them. If no automation envelopes are open, then this button will not function.

Figure 3-37

Link to Console. Engage this button to link whatever you hide or show in the Track List to the corresponding channels in Console view. Console view has a similar feature in the Banks panel, and this allows the two views to maintain a similar selection of visible tracks and channels.

Figure 3-38

Track List Presets

You can use the preset section at the bottom of the Track List to save setups for the view. Set up the view you want in the Track List, then click on the Plus icon to name and store a preset. To recall a preset, just select it from the list. To remove a preset, select it and then click on the Minus icon.

Figure 3-39

Chapter 4
RECORDING AUDIO

Basic recording is very straightforward in Studio One. This section covers the essential setup parameters and features you need to know to make sure you are ready to capture full-band or overdub sessions.

Song Setup

Check the General tab of Song Setup (Song > Song Setup) and make sure the sample rate and resolution (bit depth) are set correctly. You can also fill in song, artist and copyright details on the Meta Information tab in Song Setup.

Setting Up a Metronome Click

Enable the metronome to provide a tempo-synced click during recording using the Metronome icon on the Transport bar. Using controls at the top of each output channel in the Console, you can enable the click and adjust its level using controls.

To configure the click, open the Metronome Setup menu with the Wrench icon in the Transport bar.

Precount Bars. Determines the number of bars of click that will occur before recording starts. Usually precount is set to one or two bars to give the artist a tempo reference. Note that you still need to enable preroll (O) on the Transport bar for this to work.

Click in Precount Only. The click will play before recording only for the number of bars set in Precount Bars.

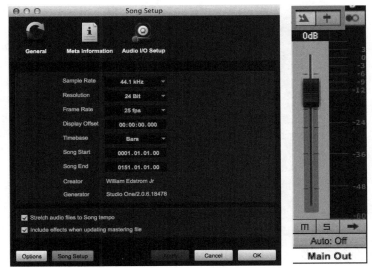

Figure 4-1

Figure 4-2

Click in Play. This option can be useful to check timing when adjusting the tempo to existing audio. If Click in Play is set to off, you won't hear the click during playback, only during recording.

Double Tempo. This means that twice as many clicks will be played. Double Tempo can be helpful for down-tempo tunes to get more clicks per bar.

Figure 4-3

Arming Tracks for Recording

In all DAWs, you need to arm (record-enable) the tracks you want to record to. In Studio One, this is done by clicking on the Record button (R) on the tracks you want to record to.

To arm several tracks at once, select the tracks and click on the Record button on one of them, or press R. It is advisable to group the tracks of multi-mic setups like drums or guitar cabinets. This way, arming one will arm the entire group without your needing to select them first.

Input Monitoring

It is important for professional recording to provide zero-latency monitoring (ZLM) for artists' headphones while tracking. Studio One works much like other DAWs in this respect but has some trick features when used with certain PreSonus audio interfaces. You can monitor through Studio One directly using the Input Monitoring button on the Track header.

Figure 4-4

Monitoring through Studio One can cause noticeable latency. For a singer this means the time delay between when you sing a note and when you hear it. You can control this by adjusting the Device Block Size setting down. But in reality, usually monitoring is best handled outside of Studio One.

Figure 4-5

Here is a breakdown of the options for creating low-latency headphone mixes.

Use the Internal Mixer in Your Audio Interface

Most audio interfaces have a virtual mixer app that allows you to set up headphone mixes with ZLM independently from your DAW software. Use this to mix mics and other inputs along with computer playback to outputs for your headphone amps. Many interfaces also allow you to add reverb, echo, and other effects to the monitor mix and offer very low latency.

When working with a separate mixer app, you need to turn off input monitoring in Studio One on the tracks. By default, input monitoring follows the state of the Record button on the track. Because of this, I recommend you disable Audio Track Monitoring Follows Record in the Options dialog box when working this way.

Use a Hardware Mixer

If you are using an analog or digital mixing console as the front end to your system, use the Sends and buses there to configure your headphone mixes. You will need to provide computer playback to the mixer via FireWire or your D/A converter to allow mixing existing tracks with the input for overdubs. You will most likely want to disable Audio Track Monitoring Follows Record in the Options dialog box for this type of setup as well.

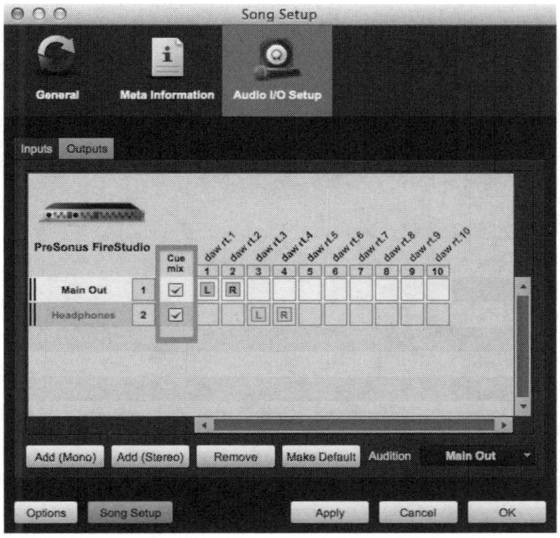

FireStudio ZLM

There are some advantages to using PreSonus brand interfaces with Studio One. PreSonus has integrated

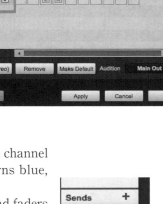

Figure 4-6

FireStudio interfaces with Studio One to provide simplified control over low-latency monitoring. To use this, check the Cue option for the outputs you want to monitor through. You can use the Main Out for ZLM, but activating it on the channel works differently as we will see shortly.

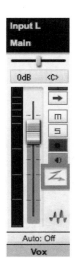

Figure 4-7

To activate ZLM for the Main Out, click on the Z next to the channel fader for any of the channels you're recording to. The Z turns blue, indicating that ZLM is active.

When Cue is chosen for outputs other than the Main Out, Send faders appear on all the channels. The Sends are located right below the inserts on each channel. To enable ZLM for these outputs, use the Z icon on the Fader Object.

The Send faders appear only if you have extra outputs and they are configured as Cue outputs in Song Setup. Enabling FireStudio ZLM bypasses any channel effects and gives Studio One direct control over the internal DSP mixer in the interfaces. You can still use Send style effects for monitoring.

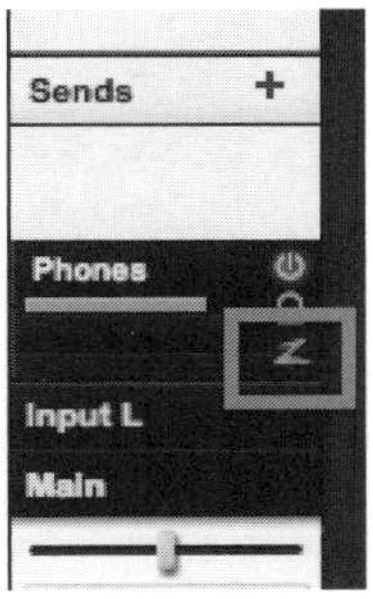

Figure 4-8

AudioBox ZLM

PreSonus USB interfaces in the AudioBox range also support integrated monitoring. These interfaces work exactly like the FireStudio ZLM described above, with one caveat—there is more latency. These interfaces don't have any hardware digital signal processing (DSP). The processing is instead handled by the computer, which can cause a few milliseconds of latency. Singers might notice a sight phasing effect in a headphone mix, but it would not typically be a problem for other musicians.

Note that some AudioBox interfaces also include a hardware mixer knob on the front panel. I tend to use this instead of the ZLM feature when tracking vocals to avoid latency.

Tape Mode

If you want Studio One to mute armed tracks during recording, enable the Audio Track Monitoring Mutes Playback (Tape Style) option in the Options dialog box. If you have ever worked with analog tape, you will probably appreciate this option.

Figure 4-9

Figure 4-10

Managing Latency

It is possible to skip all the ZLM setup options we just talked about and instead simply tune the latency of your system to be as low as possible. This can work if you have a powerful system, keep your track count lean, and avoid high-latency plug-ins while tracking.

When playing virtual instruments or guitar amp simulators, keeping the system latency as low as possible is a necessity. The key to managing latency is the Device Block Size setting in Options. This setting directly affects system latency.

Latency is the amount time the computer has to "think" before outputting sound. When playing a virtual instrument or through a guitar amp simulator, this results in a delay between when you play a note and when you hear it. An average setting is 128 or 256, but lower settings are possible. The challenge is that as you lower the setting, the computer has less time to calculate the mix and effects and might have trouble with playback. If playback results in clicks, pops, or stops, then you need to bump the Device Block Size setting back up.

Note that you can safely use higher settings for mixing or tracking if you are using one of the ZLM options explained above. This works great for recording vocals, but with amp simulators and virtual instruments, you need to monitor sound through Studio One.

On Mac, there is a setting in Options called "Process audio in safe mode (higher latency)." Usually you can run with that unchecked. If you use that option, it essentially doubles input latency.

Figure 4-11

Recording Audio

Basic recording works much as you would expect:

1. Rewind using RTZ (Comma).
2. Make sure an audio input has been assigned to each track you are recording to.
3. Enable Record for each track (N).
4. Click on Record (Numpad *) in the Transport.

That is the short version! However, there are several other settings that will give you more control over recording.

Recording with Layers

Each track can have multiple layers of audio data. Only one layer per track will be active (audible) at a time. This same concept exists by the same name in many other DAWs. Pro Tools users refer to layers as "playlists."

Loop Recording Takes to Layers

The Options dialog box and the Record Panel (View > Record Panel) have many record mode settings. Most of these are for recording with MIDI and Instrument Tracks. The most pertinent setting is Record Takes to Layers (Options > Record Takes to Layers), which you will usually leave selected. This setting is essential if you plan to use the comping tools in Studio One.

If Record Takes to Layers and loop mode (Forward Slash, or "/") are activated during recording, Studio One will automatically record a take to a layer for each pass through the loop.

After recording, all the take layers will expand with the most recent take at the top. On playback you will hear the most recent take.

Use the activate control on other another take to promote it to active. There are comprehensive controls for comping from layers that we will cover in the chapters on editing.

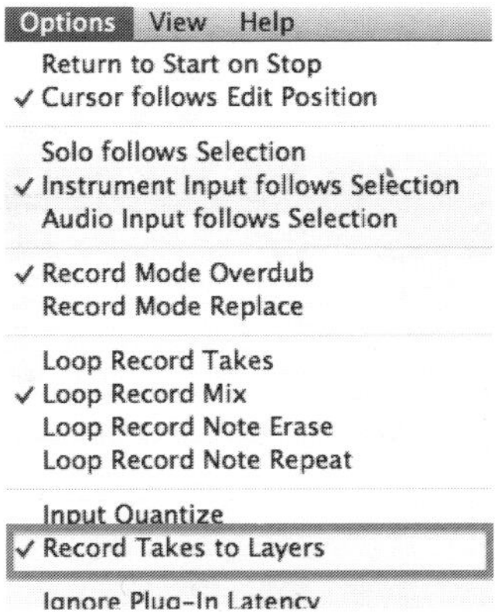

Figure 4-12

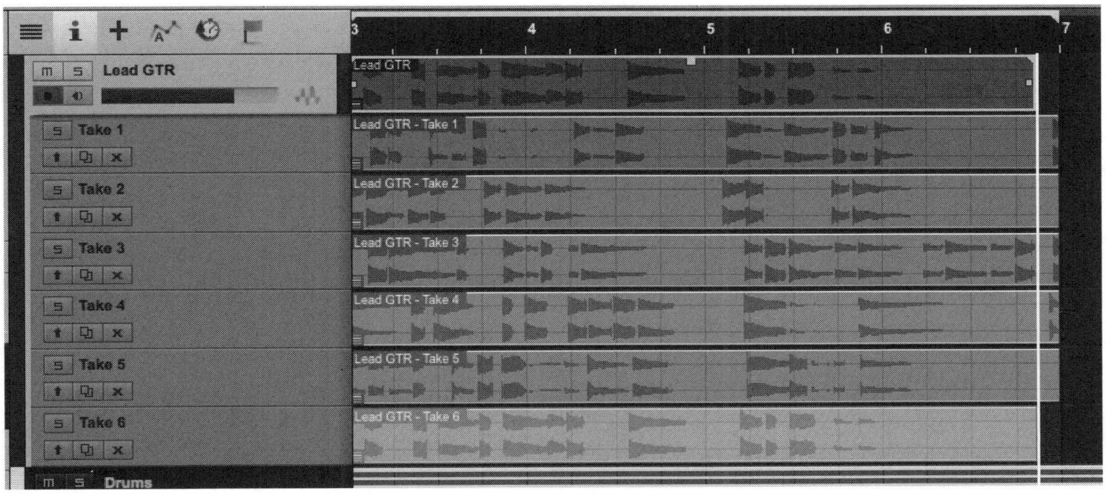

Figure 4-13

Manually Recording Takes to Layers

I often prefer to pause between takes to coach the artist before the next take, but I still want to record the takes to layers for comping. The trick to this is adding a layer (Track > Layers > Add Layer) before each new take.

By default, there is no keyboard shortcut for adding a layer. I have this assigned to the Backslash key, or "\" since it has no assignment by default. After each take, all I need to do is rewind, press "\", and start recording. If you want to simplify that further, use the Macro Toolbar to create a one-key macro to rewind, then start recording.

Loop Recording Takes to Events

If you clear the option Record Takes to Layers, new takes are recorded on top of past takes. In most cases this is probably not what you want to do. I think this feature has been retained mostly for compatibility with version 1. It is good to know what to do if you accidentally record takes this way. There is also one scenario when I still use it.

Dealing with Takes Recorded to Events

Following loop recording, right-click on the event and you will see options to convert events to tracks, new layers, or existing layers. You can also select the active take.

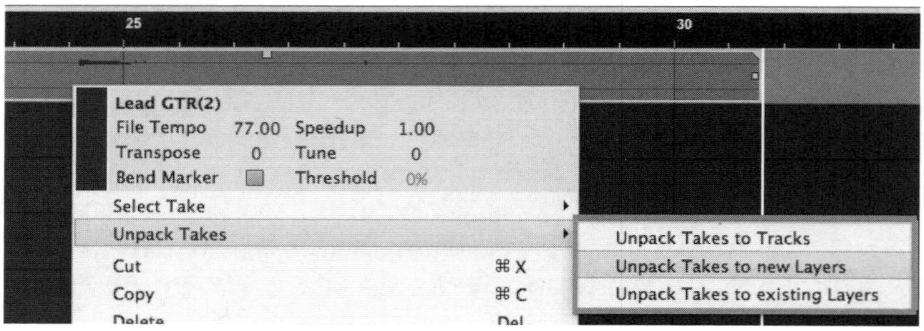

Figure 4-14

This is helpful if you have accidentally recorded takes to events or have loaded a Song recorded in an earlier version of Studio One and would now like to use the newer comping tools.

When Is Recording Takes to Events Useful?

If you are composing and writing while loop recording, this mode can be useful because it makes it possible to copy all the takes to different song sections. For example, you can loop record a chorus vocal with several takes, then copy the Event to each point in the song where a chorus occurs. Then you can unpack the takes to layers and use the comping tools to create a slightly different performance for each chorus. If you record takes to layers, when you move the active event, the underlying layers don't move.

Punch Recording

To automatically punch in and out during recording, turn Loop Active off (Forward Slash, or "/") and turn Auto Punch (I) on in the Transport bar.

Set the loop brace over the section you want replace and arm the track or tracks for recording. Position the cursor before the punch points and start

Figure 4-15

recording (Numpad *). Recording will occur only between the loop in and out points. Note that you can also manually punch in and out by engaging and disengaging Record during playback.

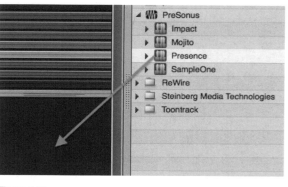

Figure 4-16

Recording Instrument Parts (MIDI)

Recording to Instrument Tracks works similarly to recording audio, except you are recording Note data into the events rather than audio. Because of this, when recording Instrument Parts you will need first to route the track output to a virtual instrument or an external MIDI sound device to hear anything.

Instrument Tracks

Create an Instrument Track by dragging a virtual instrument to the Arrange view. You can also right-click in the Track header column, select Add Instrument Track, and assign the output to a virtual instrument or MIDI output.

Recording

Assuming you have the track set up and can hear what you are playing, basic recording works like it does for audio. Simply set up the metronome, arm the track, rewind, hit Record, and start playing.

Record Panel

The Record Panel (View > Record Panel) is very helpful when recording Instrument Tracks, though the same settings are all available in the Options menu. There are a lot more modes and options for Instrument Tracks than for audio.

Figure 4-17

Record Modes

When doing straight recording—as opposed to loop recording—there are two modes to select from: Overdub and Replace.

Overdub. In Overdub mode (Options > Record Mode > Overdub), new recording passes will be merged into existing events. This gives you a MIDI version of sound-on-sound recording. An example would be to add in a missed note or cymbal crash.

Figure 4-18

Replace. Replace mode (Options > Record Mode > Replace) will adjust the length of existing events to make room for the new recording. In this mode, recording Instrument Parts works just like recording audio.

Figure 4-19

Loop Recording

When Loop Active (Forward Slash, or "/") is enabled during Instrument Track recording, there are four different recording modes. Understanding these modes is the key to efficient MIDI recording with Studio One.

Figure 4-20

Loop Record Takes. In Takes mode (Options > Loop Record Takes) a take is added for each recording pass through the loop. This works just like it does for audio recording.

Loop Record Mix. In Mix mode (Options > Loop Record Mix) each recording pass through the loop adds any new Notes you play to the previous notes. This is particularly useful when programming drumbeats. You can build the part by playing the kick on the first pass and then adding snare, hi-hat, and crashes on additional passes.

Note Erase. Use Note Erase mode (Options > Loop Record Note Erase) to remove notes. Just play the note you want to remove when you want it removed, and it will be deleted. You can also program a key on your controller to enable Note Erase. Hold down the corresponding Note on your controller to temporarily switch to the Note Erase mode.

Figure 4-21

Note Repeat. In Note Repeat mode (Options > Loop Record Note Repeat), Studio One will repeat the note for as long as you hold down the key with the frequency specified in the quantize setting. It is a quick way to enter hi-hat or dance-style parts.

Loop Recording Undo

There are two undo commands for use with loop recording. If you like to build beats with loop recording, you may wish to assign these to keyboard shortcuts. Both of these tools are designed to be used on the fly during loop recording. They are located on the Record Panel.

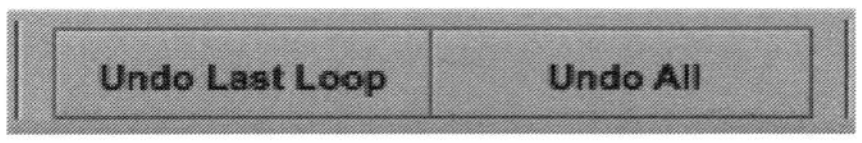

Figure 4-22

Undo Last Loop. This will remove whatever was recorded on the most recent recording pass where data was added. Additional clicks will continue to remove data until everything is gone.

Undo All. This simply clears everything you loop recorded since starting to record.

PART II: STUDIO ONE PROFESSIONAL EDITING

Chapter 5
EDITING AUDIO

Cutting, combining, pasting, chopping, duplicating, and trimming audio are central to editing in Studio One. There are also additional functions that can be used to streamline your workflow, many of which go unused by most users. Many of these core operations use the Arrow tool (shortcut key 1). There is a full suite of mouse tools that we'll cover in this chapter.

Audio Editing Basics

In Studio One, the smallest editable data element on any track is called an Event. This concept is called a Clip in most other systems. Logic calls it a Region. To become proficient in Studio One, it is essential that you understand how to work with Events.

Snap On/Off (N)

We covered the snap options in detail in chapter 1. If you are editing audio that is synced with the tempo of the song, then you will probably set the snap mode to Adaptive.

Duplicating Events

Duplicate. Studio One does not have a loop concept like Acid, SONAR, or Live, where you can pull the edge of a clip to add more repetitions. Instead, you duplicate Events for each repetition. To do this, select an Event and press D. Press repeatedly, or hold to make numerous copies of Audio Events. Duplicating an Event this way makes a copy of the underlying file, so if you make edits to the original, it has no effect on the duplicates. You will probably use this whenever you work with loops.

Shared Duplicate. There is a way to make duplicates that share the original file. To do this use Shift + D rather than D. This type of duplicate uses the same underlying file as the original.

Duplicate and Insert. Use Opt + D / Alt + D to duplicate and insert. This places the copy immediately after the original, pushing existing Events later in the song.

Info View

The Info view can load as a strip just below the Toolbar or as a floating palette. It gives you a context-sensitive summary of keyboard modifiers for mouse tools, so when you hover the tool over an Event, the Info view will show numerous options. This view helps you when you are discovering or trying to remember keyboard modifiers.

Figure 5-1

Editor View

Double-click on an Audio Event to load the Editor (F2). The Editor appears at the bottom of the screen between the Arrange view and the Transport bar. It gives you a view of all the editing tools for a single track. The Editor allows you to stay zoomed in for detailed work while keeping the Arrange view as an overview.

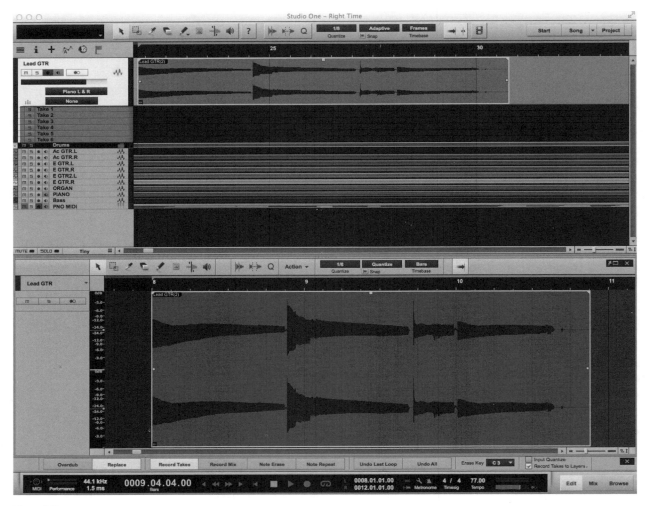

Figure 5-2

The Editor also allows you to see and edit the individual slices in Audio Parts. You can also detach the Editor, resize it, and even move it to a second monitor if you like.

Mouse Tools

There are eight mouse tools for editing Audio Events, which are selected either in the Toolbar or with keyboard numbers 1 through 8. Tool selection in Studio One works very similarly to how it does in Cubase. In addition, you can have different mouse tools active in the Arrange view and the Editor at the same time.

Many of the tool-based edit actions are influenced by the current Snap and Quantize setting. To move freely, turn off Snap to Grid (N) or temporarily override snapping by holding down the Shift key while dragging.

Figure 5-3

You will need to understand these tools to become proficient in Studio One.

Arrow Tool

Most common operations are done using the Arrow tool (shortcut key 1). Here are the primary editing actions you can do with the Arrow tool.

Move Events. Grab an Event anywhere within its boundaries and drag to reposition it or move it track to track. Track-to-track moves are automatically constrained to the original time position, so you don't need to worry that an Event moved to a new track will be out of sync.

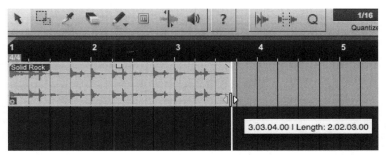

Figure 5-4

Resize (Trim). Grab the front or back edge of an Event to resize it. Many other systems would call this type of sizing "trimming." You will notice that the mouse pointer changes to the Sizing tool when you do this.

Timestretching. Holding down Opt / Alt while dragging the right edge of an Event allows you to timestretch it. The mouse pointer changes to a Timestretch tool.

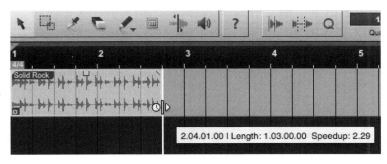

Figure 5-5

Slip Event. Slip Event ("slip editing" in other systems) allows you to move the waveform within the window of the Event. Hold down Opt + Cmd / Ctrl + Alt as you drag the waveform left or right.

Figure 5-6

Event Fades. Create a fade by dragging one of the Fade Flags. Other programs call these Fade handles.

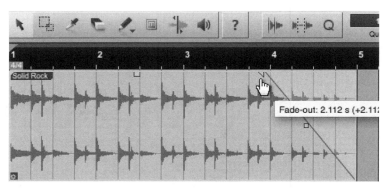

Figure 5-7

You can adjust the curve of the fade using the Fade Curve box at the center of the fade.

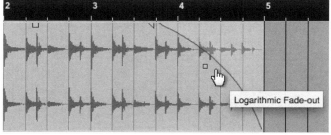

Figure 5-8

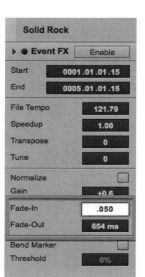

Figure 5-9

You can also adjust the fade times directly in the Event section of the Inspector.

Event Volume. To adjust the Event volume ("clip gain" in other systems), grab the Volume box at the top of the Event and drag it up or down. You can remove or add gain with this control.

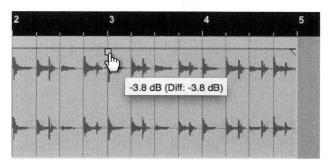

Figure 5-10

You can also adjust the gain in the Inspector for the selected Event. This type of gain adjustment happens at the Event level, before the Console or any insert effects.

Range Tool

Use the Range tool (shortcut key 2) to delete or move a section of an Event without extra split and selection steps.

Delete Range. Using the Range tool, drag over a selection of one or more Events, and press Delete. This removes the selection and leaves blank space in its place. For detailed work, you can select the range and then adjust the size of the selected area by dragging its edges. You can zoom in or use the Editor view for more accuracy.

Move Range. To quickly move a range of audio, select it with the Range tool and drag it where you want it. You can either drag it with constrained timing to another track or just move it elsewhere on the same track.

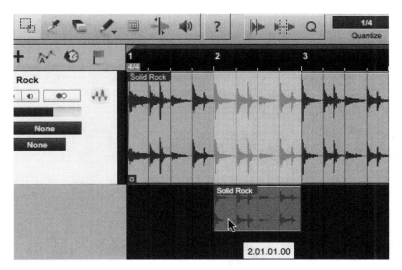

Figure 5-11

Split Tool

The Split tool (shortcut key 3) will split an Event wherever you click on it. Splitting does not position the cursor, so you can work ahead or behind the cursor even during playback.

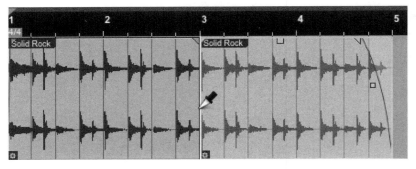

Figure 5-12

If you have Snap to Grid (N) enabled, all splits will happen on the grid. This makes editing much easier. You can temporarily switch to the Arrow tool when the Split tool is selected by holding down Cmd / Ctrl.

Eraser Tool

With the Eraser tool (shortcut key 4) selected, click on any Event to erase it. You can also erase numerous events by swiping across them.

Paint Tool

Drag over a track with the Paint tool (shortcut key 5) to create a blank Audio Event. This is occasionally useful with audio editing for creating a dummy event or placeholder. For the most part, the Paint tool is used for editing automation or drawing in notes, but we'll get to that later.

Mute Tool

Click on an Event with the Mute tool (shortcut key 6) to mute it. Click again to unmute. Muted Events appear gray and won't play any sound. You can also swipe across numerous Events to mute or unmute them.

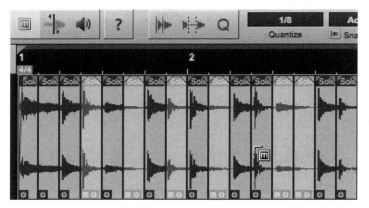

Figure 5-13

Bend Tool

Use the Bend tool (shortcut key 7) to insert or move Bend Markers. This tool is for the Audio Bend feature that will be covered later in this chapter.

Listen Tool

The Listen tool (shortcut key 8) will solo playback from wherever you click on it and hold. It is a helpful shortcut when auditioning takes and tracks for comping. I will cover comping later in this chapter.

Editing Multiple Events at Once

You can do most editing operations on more than one Event at the same time. Just select the Events by dragging over them with the Arrow tool or Shift-click to add additional Events to the selection. This works great for resizing or adjusting fades across Events or tightening up sliced drumbeats.

You can edit Events on more than one track at the same time if the tracks are assigned to the same group. This is useful when editing multitrack drums.

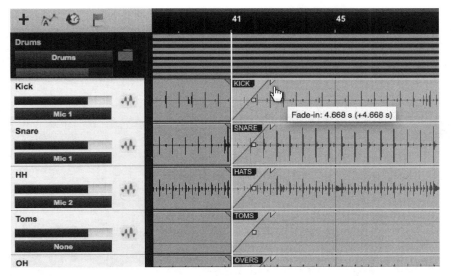

Figure 5-14

To group tracks, select the tracks to group and hit Cmd + G / Ctrl + G. If the tracks are already in a Folder Track, you can use the Group button in the Folder Track header to quickly group them.

Crossfades

Crossfading between two Events is the same as fading one Event out as another fades in. This is fine as an effect, but with audio editing it is often done over just a few milliseconds to prevent pops and clicks. Crossfades are used extensively when editing drums, and all these techniques work the same on grouped tracks as they do on individual Events.

Creating Crossfades

Select two adjacent or overlapping Events and press X. This will instantly create a crossfade. If there are Events on each side of an Event, pressing X will create crossfades on both sides.

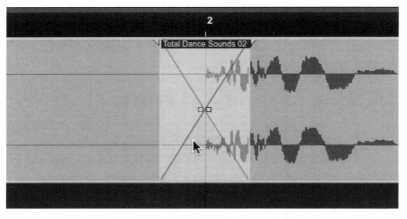

Figure 5-15

Adjusting Crossfades

To adjust the width of a crossfade, drag either Fade Flag left or right. To adjust the fade curve, drag either Fade Curve box up or down. You can configure linear, exponential or logarithmic crossfade curves this way.

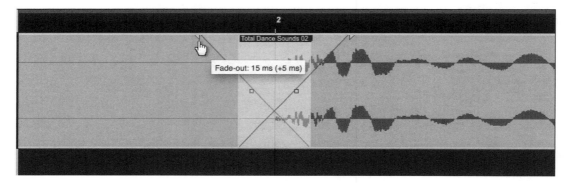

Figure 5-16

Moving Crossfades

Move the mouse to the center of the crossfade and drag left or right. This allows you to position the entire crossfade accurately. This is great when adjusting crossfades to occur just before the transient.

Splitting

Splitting Events into two or more is essential to editing digital audio. Studio One offers several ways to get this action done.

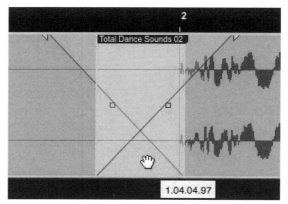

Figure 5-17

Split at Grid

It is possible to chop an Event based on the grid without repeatedly clicking on the Split tool. To do this, set up the grid increment in the Quantize property and select Split at Grid (Event > Split at Grid). This command is also available from the right-click menu for Events.

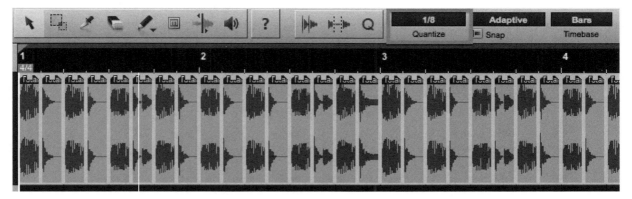

Figure 5-18

Locate and Split

Studio One, like many other DAWs, allows you to split using keyboard commands. To do this, use the Arrow tool to point where you want to split an event. Press Cmd + Spacebar / Ctrl + Spacebar. This puts the cursor wherever you were pointing. (Note: Mac users will need to disable or reassign the Spotlight menu keyboard shortcut in System Preferences > Spotlight for this shortcut to work.) Then, press Opt + X / Alt + X to split at the cursor.

The Tab key will move the cursor to the next transient on the selected track. This tab-to-transient feature can help you get the cursor right where it needs to be before using Split at Cursor.

Audio Bend Panel Slice

We haven't covered Audio Bend yet, but it is worth mentioning that the Bend panel has a Split option. Using the Audio Bend tools, you can detect transients and adjust Bend Markers. Usually you use this with Quantize to adjust timing by using timestretching. You also have the options to just slice up the waveform at the Bend Markers. It is another cool and useful way to split Audio Events. We will cover this in more detail a bit later in the chapter.

Figure 5-19

Moving Split Points

Position the mouse pointer between two adjacent Events on the lower third of the waveform, and drag left or right to reposition a split point. The mouse pointer will be represented as a Double Arrow sizing tool.

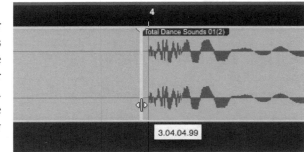

Figure 5-20

Comping

Studio One has an easy-to-use system for comping, or creating a composite from several takes. Usually, this is used to assemble a lead or solo from the best parts of multiple takes.

Preparing for Comping

To use the comping feature, all the takes must be organized into layers on the track. If you record the takes to layers, this is done automatically.

If you recorded takes to individual tracks, then you will need to consolidate them as layers on one track. To do this, create a new blank track where you will build the composite. Drag all the Events of the last take to the new track. Add a new layer (Track > Layers > Add Layer). (You will probably want to create a keyboard shortcut for this. I use Backslash, "\".) Drag the next take into the new layer. Create a new layer and continue until all the takes are in layers. Expand the layers so you can see all the takes with the right-click command in the Track header.

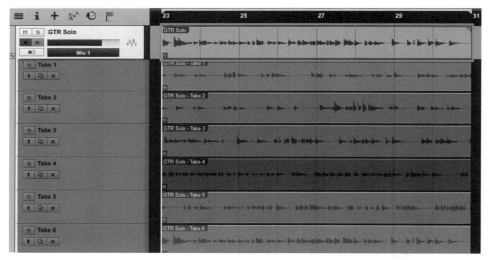

Figure 5-21

Figure 5-22

Following loop recording, the active (top) layer is a copy of the final take. In Figure 5-21, the highlighted Event is a copy of Take 6. I usually delete this copy before I start comping. The composite will be assembled onto the top layers.

Before comping it is a very good idea to save a new version of your Song (File > Save New Version). Enter a note that says something like "before comping lead vocal." This way you can always return the Song to its state prior to comping if things go wrong and you need to start over.

How Comping Works

Make any layer active by clicking on the Activate Layer button on each take. Use this feature along with the Listen tool to audition all the takes.

Use the Listen tool (8), select it, then click-and-hold right before any phrase. This lets you listen to just that phase without needing to activate it or mute other tracks. This is a huge time-saver when comping.

Figure 5-23

Figure 5-24

Use the Arrow tool (1) to swipe over sections or phrases that you want as part of the composite. The swiped range will be instantly copied to the active layer as part of the composite. Continue until you are happy with the assembled composite.

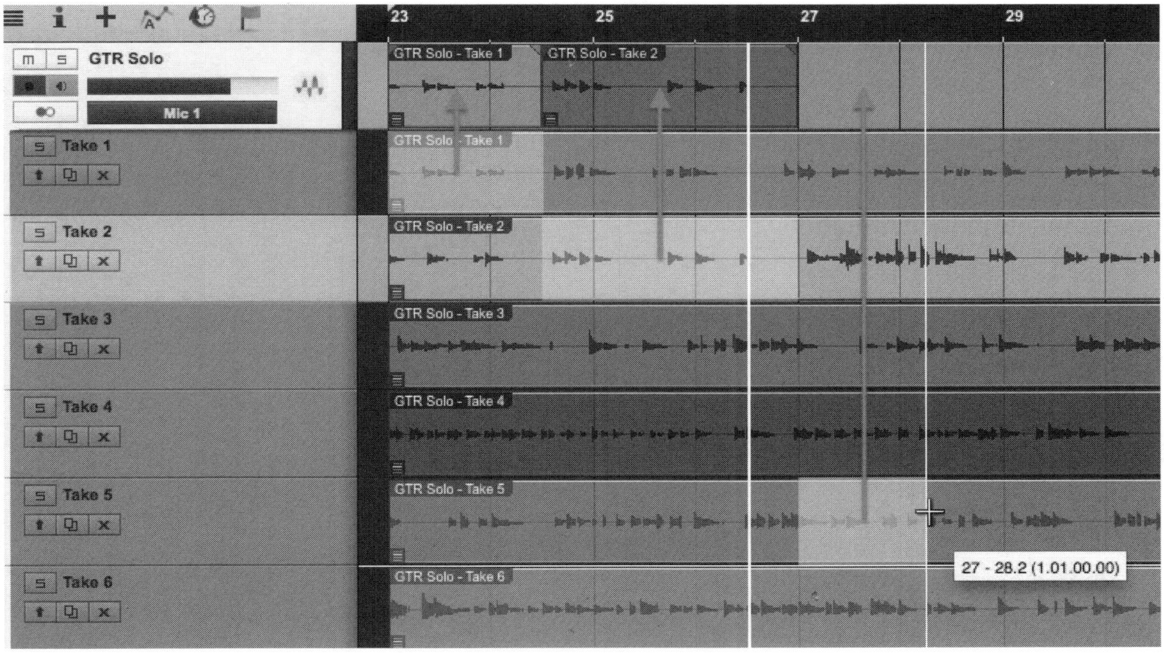

Figure 5-25

You can also edit the Events that make up the composite using all the normal mouse tools and techniques to adjust timing, change Event volume, or create crossfades. When you are finished with the composite, you might want to bounce the Events (Cmd + B / Ctrl + B) to a single Event and turn off Expand Layers to hide the takes.

Chapter 6
AUDIO BEND
AND QUANTIZE

Audio Bend in Studio One is similar to "elastic audio" in Pro Tools, "audio warp" in Cubase, "audio snap" in SONAR, and "flex audio" in Logic. In short, it allows you to add Bend Markers before the transients automatically via detection or manually with the Bend tool. With Bend Markers in place you can adjust timing manually or by quantizing. The Studio One implementation of Zplane Élastique makes the timestretching very smooth. In fact, it outperforms many of the established DAWs.

Audio Bend

Audio Bend involves timestretching, which resamples the audio to make it faster or slower without changing the pitch. Though it is a great feature, it will always degrade the audio somewhat. Because of this, although it is useful, Audio Bend is not necessarily the best choice for all situations. Timing corrections can also be made using standard editing techniques like splitting, moving, and crossfading.

Audio Bend allows an almost magical way of quantizing audio that was previously possible only with MIDI. While most demos show quickly analyzing the audio and applying quantization, checking the results and tweaking Bend Marker placement first produce the best results. And remember you don't actually need to do any auto quantizing with Audio Bend—you can manually bend just the spots in the track with timing problems. I cover manual bending at the end of this chapter.

In addition, the Audio Bend panel has an option to just split the track into separate Events on each transient. This isn't bending at all, but is a useful tool, nonetheless.

Bend Panel

Audio Bend editing can be done in the Arrange view or the Editor and works essentially the same way in both views. To access Audio Bend functions, open the Bend panel using the button on the Toolbar. Another way is to find View > Additional Views > Audio Bend on the menu.

Figure 6-1

To use Audio Bend follow a workflow from left to right using the Detection, Bend Marker, Track, and Action tools in the Bend panel. Let's take a look at the Audio Bend workflow.

Audio Bend Detection

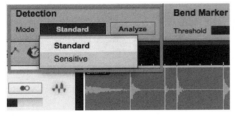

Figure 6-2

Select one or more Events, set the mode to Standard, and click on Analyze. Blue markers will appear before the transients throughout the Event.

Adjust the sensitivity of detection using the Threshold slider. If lower-level transients are not getting picked up, change the mode to Sensitive and click on Analyze again. Now, when you adjust the Threshold slider, lower-level transients will be indicated.

Note that you can also initiate transient detection from the Audio section of the right-click menu or the Action menu in the Editor.

Magnifying the waveform with the Data Zoom slider can be very helpful when adjusting the Threshold to make sure you are picking up the weaker transients. Data Zoom is located in the lower-right corner of the Arrange view.

About Bend Markers

Bend Markers appear as light-blue vertical lines positioned at the transients in an Event following detection. To work with Bend Markers, select the Bend tool from the Toolbar.

Figure 6-3

If you click on a Bend Marker with the Bend tool, it turns yellow indicating that it has been selected. To select a range of Bend

Figure 6-4

Markers, hold down Opt / Alt and drag with the Bend tool. You can drag Bend Markers left or right to adjust timing using timestretching. I will go over the details of editing Bend Markers shortly.

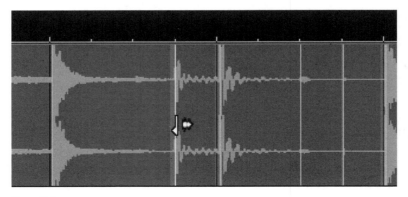

Figure 6-5

When you select a Bend Marker, you might see a directional arrow flag at the bottom of the marker. If the transient has been moved, this arrow will point back toward the original Timeline position. As you drag a marker across the original position, the arrow will flip to the other side much like a guitar tuner. You can always reset the Bend Marker from the right-click menu.

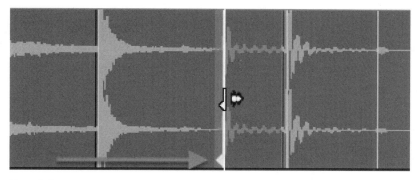

Figure 6-6

Studio One Bend Markers don't do any bending to the leading edge of transients. This is how it retains the natural character of drums and percussion. The part of the transient that has no timestretching applied is indicated with in light-blue shading.

Here is a rundown of things you can do when editing, positioning, and moving Bend Markers.

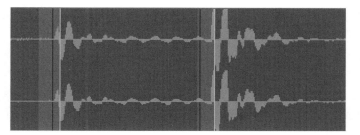

Figure 6-7

Show/Hide Bend Markers

You can hide Bend Markers using the Bend Marker box in the Bend panel. This doesn't remove them. It just hides them and all the other color coding related to bending. The same control will toggle Bend Markers back on. Note that you can also toggle the Bend Markers from the Event right-click menu or the Event properties in the Inspector.

Remove Bend Markers

To remove a single Bend Marker, just double-click on it with the Bend tool. Delete is also available on the right-click menu.

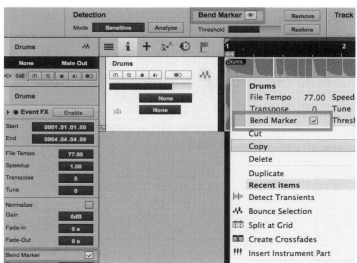

Figure 6-8

Figure 6-9

Figure 6-10

Click on the Remove button in the Bend panel to remove all Bend Markers. This effectively clears the analysis and manual changes you have made with Audio Bend. Use this if you decide you don't want to use Audio Bend or you just want to clear out your experiments and start over.

Reset Bend Markers

To reset any Bend Marker, right-click on it using the Bend tool and choose Reset Bend Marker. This works for single Bend Markers or a selection of markers.

Figure 6-11

The Restore button clears any quantize or manual timing changes, basically resetting the timing for all Bend Markers for the selected Event. It doesn't remove the Event markers. Note: The Restore button is not an undo for the Remove button!

Selecting Multiple Bend Markers

Select a Bend Marker, then hold down Shift as you select additional markers. Changes will then apply to the selection rather than just one marker.

Another way to select multiple markers is by holding down Opt / Alt and dragging over markers. This even works across tracks, which helps for cleaning extraneous markers from fills in multitrack drums.

Audio Bend Track Options

The track options give you more control over bending, particularly when using multitrack drums. You can often use the defaults here for most single-event bending.

Figure 6-12

Timestretch

For most Audio Bend operations, Timestretch should be set to Audio Bend. This property sets the timestretching algorithm for the track and is the very same thing as the Timestretch property in the Inspector for the track.

Figure 6-13

The main purpose of this value is to verify that the track is set to Audio Bend. You can try the other algorithms for slightly different results, but Audio Bend is usually the best bet.

Group

The Group property allows you to assign selected tracks to a group or remove them from a group. You can do exactly the same thing from the Inspector, and this property is really repeated here for convenience.

Figure 6-14

When bending something like an overdubbed background vocal, I often want to remove it from a group temporarily. For drums, on the other hand, it is usually advisable to keep the tracks grouped to make sure the edits happen across all tracks to avoid phasing issues.

Guides

Use the Guides drop-down list to select which tracks from the current group will be used as guide tracks for Audio Bend. This is really intended for multitrack drums but can be used for any multiple-microphone situation.

For drums, I often select one kick and one snare track as guides for transient detection. Bending for all the other drum tracks will follow along. This avoids the phasing problems, since the same signal is picked up by several mics when recording a drum kit. Sometimes I use the overhead mics as guides for drums, but honestly, it depends on the mix approach.

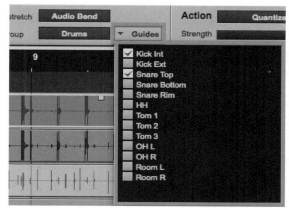

Figure 6-15

Audio Bend Actions

The final section of the Bend panel is where you choose what to do with all the Bend Markers. Audio Bend is really all about helping you quantize audio, but you can also slice up the Event at each transient to prepare for other kinds of editing.

The options are different, depending on if you select Quantize or Slice. Let's look at both.

Bend Action Quantize

Set the action to Quantize, adjust the Strength slider, and click on Apply. Studio One will use all the Bend Markers to stretch the audio so that the transients snap to the grid currently defined by the Quantize setting in the Toolbar.

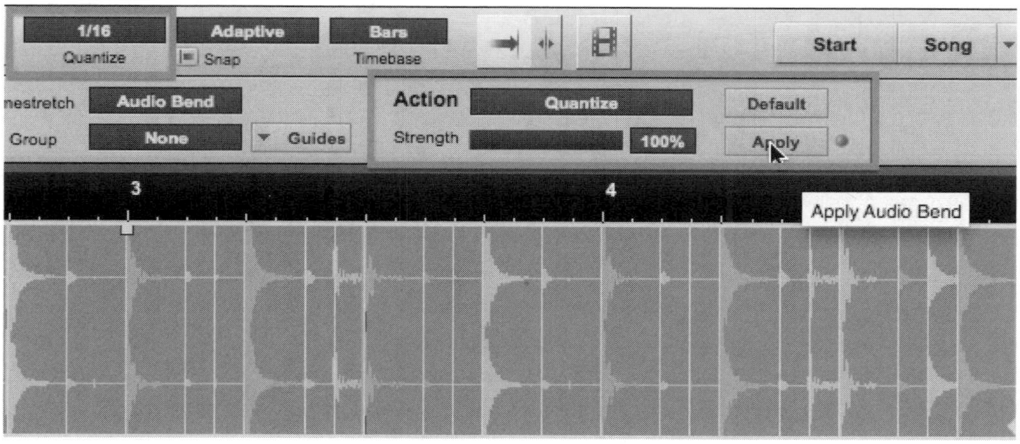

Figure 6-16

The Strength property determines how closely each Bend Marker is pulled to the grid. So if you want to completely tighten the timing, set Strength to 100%. Note that the Bend Panel Strength value is the same thing as the Quantize Panel Start value.

Bend Action Slice

When you click on Apply, with Action set to Slice, the Event will be split at each Bend Marker. This is a very helpful tool for chopping up beats.

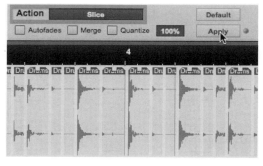

Figure 6-17

The Slice action has three other options: Autofades, Merge, and Quantize. You can select any or all of these options to tweak the results of slicing:

Figure 6-18

Autofades. Choose Autofades to automatically apply short fade-ins and fade-outs to each resulting slice to eliminate clicks and pops that might occur when slices are moved or quantized.

Merge. Merge combines all the resulting slices into one Audio Part. This makes sliced audio much easier to manage. All the individual slices are still available to edit in the Editor view.

Quantize. Choose the Quantize option and value to automatically quantize the beginnings of each resulting Event slice. This doesn't do any timestretching, but instead moves the slices to line up with the grid. The Quantize value sets the strength of this action. This works much like the Quantize on Track command (Event > Quantize > Quantize on Track).

The Bend panel and Quantize panel are related. If you want more control over quantizing, switch to the Quantize panel after you have the Bend Markers defined. You will find more options for swing and musical divisions than you will find in the Quantize property of the Toolbar.

Applying Audio Bend Actions

Figure 6-19

The function of Apply is pretty obvious—it makes quantizing happen. However, I want to point out the function of the blue indicator light.

Once you click on Apply, a blue indicator light will appear next to the button. As long as you don't change the selection of Events, this indicator means you can try changes to the Audio Bend settings without using undo first. This allows you to try different settings quickly and experiment with the options. This saves time, since Audio Bend often requires a degree of trial and error.

Manual Audio Bend

To me, manually adjusting timing is one of the most useful, yet overlooked approaches for making timing corrections for professionals. It gives you control, with much less work than older cut-and-splice methods. It also puts you in charge of exactly how bending should take place, rather than leaving it up to an algorithm.

Here are the steps to manually bend to adjust timing:

1. Set the track Timestretch mode to Audio Bend in the Inspector.
2. Turn on Bend Markers for the Audio Events on the track by right-clicking on the Events and checking the Bend Marker box.
3. Select the Bend tool and click on where you want to place a Bend Marker.
4. Adjust the position of the Bend Marker by holding Opt / Alt as you drag left or right. This helps you place it right before the transient.
5. Drag the Bend Marker left or right to bend the audio to correct or change the timing.

> **Tip:** When using a manual bend approach, you might want to insert Bend Markers before and after the section you are working on to prevent audio from being stretched outside the current song section or bars.

Audio Quantize

We have already seen that you can quantize audio using the Bend panel. You can also quantize with other tools in Studio One.

Quick Quantize

You can quickly quantize audio to the grid. Simply select one or more Events and hit Q. This analyzes the audio, inserts Bend Markers, and quantizes in a single action. This works well for audio with a good level and clear transients. For lots of material it is sort of hit or miss. I usually prefer the control of using the Bend panel and careful Bend Marker placement, but if Q works, it's like magic.

Quantize Panel

The Quantize panel opens up many more options for quantizing audio. Some of the features are specific to Instrument Parts and will be covered later. Open the Quantize panel using the button on the Toolbar or View > Additional Views > Quantize.

Figure 6-20

The panel is divided into three primary sections that give you all the properties to define quantizing. The sections are not labeled but follow the quantize setup from left to right. Let's go over each section and the quantize workflow.

Define the Quantize Grid

The first two buttons on the Quantize panel offer two completely different ways to define the quantize grid:

Grid. With Grid selected, use the Note Value and Swing options to define the grid. There are a few more options here than on the Toolbar, including Quintole, Septole, and a variable swing amount.

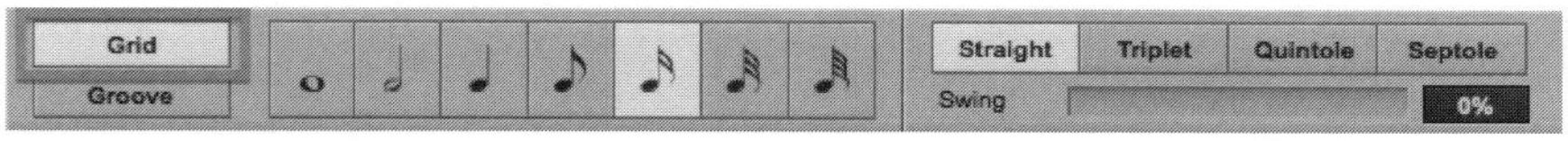

Figure 6-21

Groove. With Groove selected, you can set the grid to match any note pattern. You can drag in any Instrument Part or even audio, and the groove will be extracted and used as the quantize grid.

Figure 6-22

> **Tip:** Though it's not obvious, you can actually drag a groove from the Groove bin back into the arrangement. This will give you an Instrument Part that you can use as the timing base for creating additional tracks.

Many other programs allow you to quantize to preset grooves. Studio One simplifies this by allowing you to groove quantize to almost anything.

Define the Quantize Strength

The middle section of the Quantize panel offers four different strength values:

Figure 6-23

Start. Start is essentially quantize strength. This determines how perfectly Studio One moves transients toward the grid.

End and Velocity. End and Velocity apply only to Instrument Parts, so we will go over those when we talk about editing Notes and MIDI.

Range. Range sets how close to grid divisions snapping will occur. At 100% this value has no effect. As you lower the value, Notes further from the grid are no longer corrected.

Quantize Actions and Setups

The final section offers some shortcuts for working with commonly used quantize settings and buttons to invoke quantizing. On lower-resolution screens this section might not appear. If you don't see it, try opening the Quantize panel as a floating window.

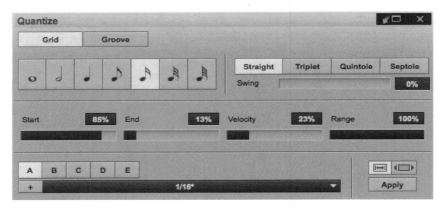

Figure 6-24

Figure 6-25

Quantize Setups. You can store quick access presets for quantize setups in registers A through E. Simply select one of the registers and configure the options. If you move to a different register and back, the setup will remain. This feature is simpler than it appears; there is no save or confirm, just five different workspaces for your quantize settings.

Quantize Presets. Presets allow you to save configurations of the Quantize panel to disc. You can then recall a favorite configuration into different Songs. Note that when you save a preset it saves only the current register, not the entire set of five registers.

Figure 6-26

Quantize. The Quantize option is the normal mode for quantizing. When you click on Apply in this mode, Studio One uses Audio Bend to move Note beginnings to line up with the grid. This is the very same thing that happens when you hit the keyboard shortcut Q.

Quantize on Track. Quantize on Track is used to quantize Event beginnings rather than bending based on transients. This is useful only for chopped-up audio, which is typical with drumbeats. It is also a great way to quantize if you applied the Split mode in the Bend panel.

Apply. Apply is the final step. If you use quantizing a lot, you will get used to just hitting Q.

Figure 6-27

Multitrack Audio Bend

One of the common issues producers and engineers face is correcting timing on multitrack drum recordings. This is a necessary step for current pop and country production trends. The challenge is to get tight drum edits that sound natural without spending hours and hours in the editing process. Studio One Folder Tracks, Audio Bend, and the Quantize panel come together to give you great-sounding results with a very efficient workflow. This approach uses timestretching to adjust timing. This is a parallel concept to Pro Tools' "elastic audio."

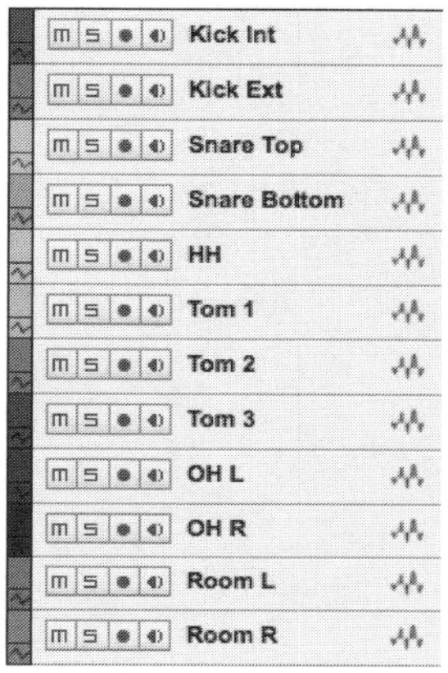

Figure 6-28

Setup

Here is a step-by-step for correcting or tightening the timing on multitrack drums:

1. **Set the Track Order.** Make sure your drum track names are clear and in a correct order.

2. **Bounce Events.** If they are not continuous Events, bounce them down so there is one Event per track with the command Cmd + B / Ctrl + B.

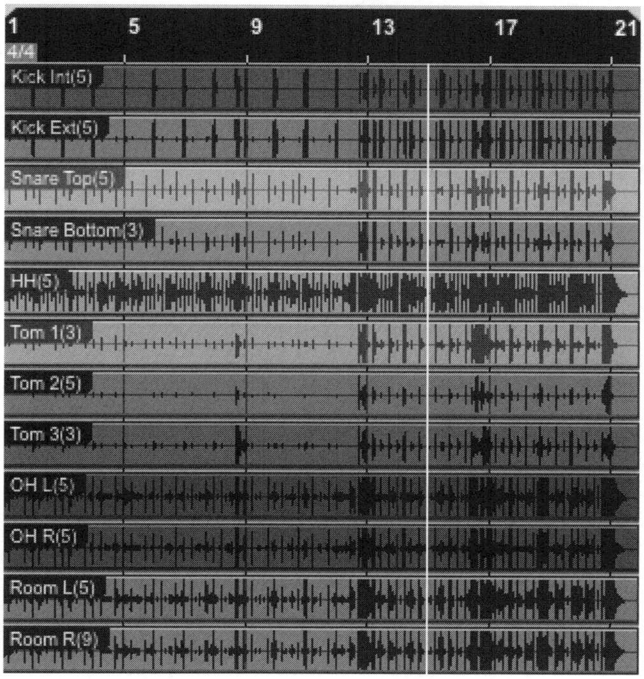

Figure 6-29

Figure 6-30

3. **Pack Folder.** Pack tracks to a Folder Track, and then group the drums. Folder Tracks are a real advantage here, because you can quickly group and ungroup the drums.

Access this option by right-clicking on the selected tracks and then clicking on Pack Folder.

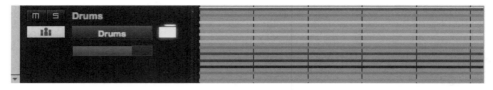

Figure 6-31

4. **Select the Guide Tracks.** The Guides drop-down list in the Track section of the Audio Bend panel lets you pick which tracks are used as the Bend reference. You can't quantize to all transients across all mics because of phase issues. More distant mics will be delayed if they are stretched to match the drums—all kinds of phase cancellations will happen. Most of the time selecting the snare and kick provides the best results.

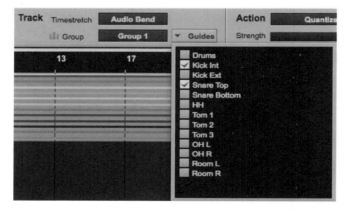

Figure 6-32

Sometimes I also add the hi-hat mic if I need those transients. Other times it works well to use just the overhead mics as guides. Fortunately it is easy to experiment with this to find which guides give you the best results.

5. **Detect Transients.** Analyze the audio and adjust the Threshold control. I usually start in Standard mode and focus on the transients of the guide tracks, making sure it's picking up all the main snare and kick hits.

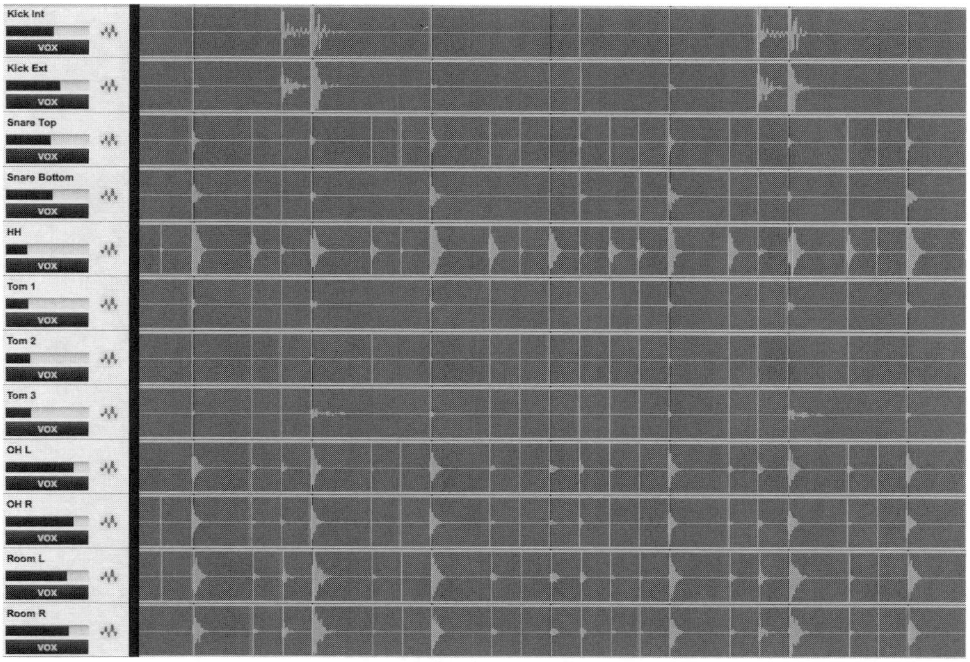

Figure 6-33

6. **Set the Quantize Grid.** This value depends on the music, but setting for sixteenth notes is often a good starting point. For more control, switch to the Quantize panel and use the additional musical options there.

Figure 6-34

7. **Set the Quantize Strength.** I almost always start with Strength at 100% for my initial trials. After I have verified that the quantizing is working, I back off that value. To make editing easier, I want the transients to fall just after the grid divisions. I find that 80 to 85% often works really well for this.

8. **Click on Apply.** Check the results. You can adjust the settings and click on apply again. In most cases, it is not necessary to undo (Cmd + Z / Ctrl + Z) before trying a new setup.

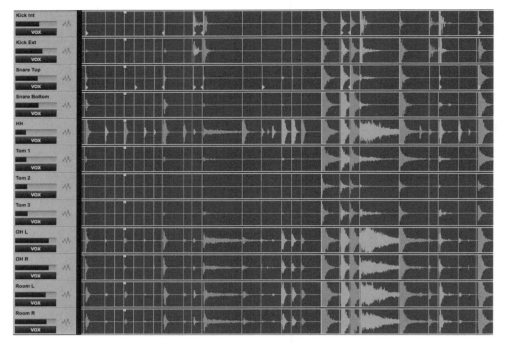

Figure 6-35

If the bending sounds unnatural during fills, you might try removing all the Bend Markers during the fill. Just hold down Opt / Alt to select Bend Markers across all the tracks and then delete.

The Studio One bending is so smooth that this process provides excellent, usable results. In addition, you can use this to change the feel of an existing drum part. For example, try adding a bit of swing to a steady tempo beat.

If you set the Action in the Audio Bend panel to Slice you can split the tracks into Events based on the transients of the guide tracks. This is similar to using Pro Tools' Beat Detective. There will typically be much more cleanup and manual editing with the Slice method, but the option is there if you prefer that type of workflow.

Chapter 7
MELODYNE
INTEGRATION

Melodyne is an amazing tool for pitch correction. It gives you a great deal of control over pitch, formats, and the pitch envelope, yet remains easy to use. For many pitch correction tasks, Melodyne surpasses the industry-standard Auto-Tune. While Auto-Tune works just fine in Studio One, Melodyne is deeply integrated with Studio One, using technology codeveloped between PreSonus and Celemony, called ARA (Figure 7-1).

Figure 7-1

ARA is short for "Audio Random Access." This gives you seamless access to Melodyne right in Studio One. It also means that Melodyne has immediate access to the underlying files for Audio Events, so there is no intermediate resampling of the audio before pitch correction can begin.

Melodyne is available in three versions: Essential, Assistant, and Editor. Find a comparison chart to see which version would be best for you by using the link in Figure 7-2.

A license for Melodyne Essential is included with Studio One, but the more full-featured versions are integrated if you have the upgraded license. I have used the full Melodyne Editor for years, and it is a fantastic tool for pitch and time manipulations. Even so, most common pitch editing tasks can be done with Essential. Melodyne Essential has only a single editing tool, called the Main tool.

Figure 7-2

Figure 7-3

This same tool is included with Melodyne Editor, along with a full palette of others.

Figure 7-4

Editor also includes the amazing Direct Note Access (DNA) technology that lets you make pitch changes to notes within a chord. It is certainly a worthy upgrade to make if you don't already have it!

For this section I will use the features available in Melodyne Essential. Everything you learn here will also translate to the other versions.

Installation

Melodyne Essential is a separate download and install from Studio One > Studio One Installation. You will need to register the software at the Celemony site. If you already own Melodyne Assistant or Editor, there is nothing you need to do except make sure you have installed the latest version.

All	New Content	Installed Content	Third Party
☐	**Synth Session** (1.81 GB, 30:00 min)		Installed on: 13.1.2012 11:58:50
☐	**Studio One Impulse Responses** (1.11 GB, 18:00 min)		Installed on: 13.1.2012 11:58:50
☐	**Electronic Kits and Musicloops** (280.00 MB, 4:00 min)		Installed on: 13.1.2012 11:58:50
☐	**Studio One FX** (520.00 MB, 8:00 min)		Installed on: 13.1.2012 11:58:50
➡	**Celemony Melodyne Essential** (248.00 MB, 4:00 min)		
➡	**Native Instruments Komplete Elements** (3.37 GB, 57:00 min)		

Figure 7-5

Figure 7-6

Using Melodyne

In this section I will introduce basic editing with Melodyne. For more details on Melodyne, check out some excellent video tutorials on Melodyne Essential available for free at the Celemony website (Figure 7-6).

Editing with Melodyne

To use Melodyne, right-click on an Audio Event and select Edit with Melodyne from the context menu (Audio > Edit with Melodyne). It is also available through the Action menu in the Editor, or with the shortcut Cmd + M / Ctrl + M. This will open the Melodyne view below the Arrange view. The Melodyne window can be undocked, resized, or moved to a second monitor and expanded to full-screen view.

Audio Processing	
Normalize Audio	⌥ N
Reverse Audio	⌘ R
Strip Silence	
Edit with Melodyne	⌘ M
Remove Melodyne	⌥⌘ M
Volume Envelope	
Create Autofades	⇧ X

Figure 7-7

> **Tip:** Melodyne works at the Audio Event level, so if your lead vocal track is broken up into multiple events, you probably want to bounce it down to a single event first.

Removing Melodyne

To remove Melodyne from an Audio Event, right-click on the event and select Remove Melodyne from the context menu (Audio > Remove Melodyne). You can also remove Melodyne with Opt + Cmd + M / Alt + Ctrl + M.

Note that Melodyne loads in the Event FX bin in the Inspector. It can also be removed or rendered like any other Event FX.

Choosing the Algorithm

When you choose Edit with Melodyne, it automatically selects between Melodic or Percussive. Polyphonic is shown but is only available with Melodyne Editor. You can override the detected algorithm very simply:

Figure 7-8

Navigating the Melodyne Edit View

The Melodyne view has its own style that is a bit different from Studio One, but many of the basics are similar:

Position the Cursor. Click in the upper part of the Melodyne Timeline ruler to position the cursor. Studio One will follow along. It works the other way around, too. Note that Melodyne does not use the Snap setting or Quantize value from Studio One.

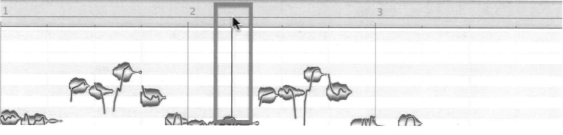

Figure 7-9

Set the Loop. Drag over the lower part of the Melodyne Timeline ruler to set the loop in and out points. In Studio One you drag over the top part of the Timeline to set the loop, so this takes a bit of adjustment. Regardless, the loop setting is automatically synced between both. Melodyne documentation refers to this topic as "cycle editing."

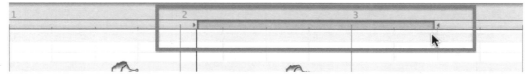

Figure 7-10

Zoom In and Out. Horizontal zooming in Melodyne works very much like it does in Studio One. Just drag up or down on the top part of the Timeline ruler. Another way to zoom horizontally is with the zoom controls at each end of the scrollbar at the bottom of the Melodyne view. Dragging the Zoom tool left and right over the editing area is yet another way to zoom.

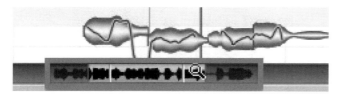

Figure 7-11

Tip: Double-click in the center of the horizontal or vertical scrollbar "thumbs" to set the screen to contain all Blobs. This is a quick way to reset zoom if you lose track of the data.

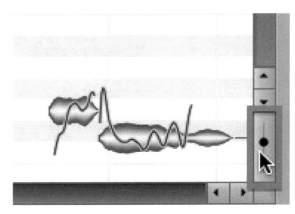

Figure 7-12

Data Zoom. Make the note Blobs bigger using the slider at the lower right. This is essentially a Data Zoom.

Transport Controls. Most Studio One Transport controls work the same in Melodyne. Use the Spacebar or double-click in the Timeline to play or pause. Use Comma to rewind or the Numpad numbers to position by markers.

Blobs and the Main Tool

Notes in Melodyne are represented as Blobs. The Edit view for Melodyne looks much like a MIDI piano-roll view with Blobs in place of MIDI notes. Blobs are located along the Timeline aligned to pitches represented along the vertical axis. The Main tool acts as a smart tool—the function changes depending on where you grab the Blob. The best way to see this is to turn on Show Blob Info.

Figure 7-13

The Main tool is a bit like the Arrow tool in the rest of Studio One. You use it to move a Blob forward or backward in time, change the length, or drag vertically to change the pitch. With Show Blob Info on, you can see that each Blob is divided into four zones as you hover the pointer over it. Here are the details for each zone:

Figure 7-14

1. **Center Zone—Move/Pitch.** Drag a Blob from the center up or down to adjust pitch or left or right to adjust timing. The cursor appears as an Arrow. Once you start dragging vertically, you need to release the mouse button before you can drag horizontally and vice versa. Add Opt / Alt as you drag up and down to override pitch snapping.
2. **Upper Zone—Split.** Double-click anywhere along the upper edge to split the Blob into two parts. The cursor appears as a Split tool.

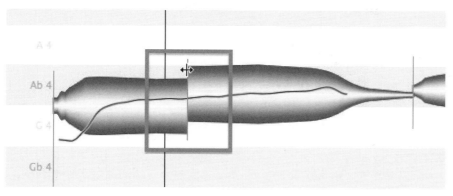

Figure 7-15

3. **Left Zone—Stretch/Compress from the Beginning.** Grab and drag the left zone left or right to stretch or compress the note. This adjusts the beginning of the Blob while leaving ending and transition to the next Note anchored. The cursor appears as a stretch pointer.

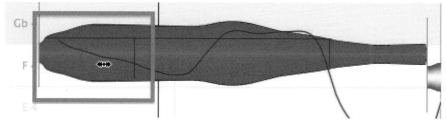

Figure 7-16

4. **Right Zone—Stretch/Compress from the Ending.** Grab the right zone to stretch or compress a Blob from the end leaving the front of the note in place. The cursor appears as a stretch pointer.

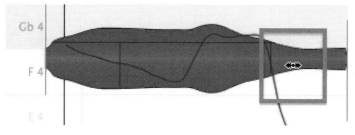

Figure 7-17

Pitch Snap

Melodyne has some great tools to help you tune tracks to chromatic or other scales. Turn on Chromatic Snap or Scale Snap from the drop-down menu in the upper left corner of the Melodyne Edit view or from the menu (Edit > Pitch Grid). If you choose Chromatic Snap, snapping will be set to the nearest semitone.

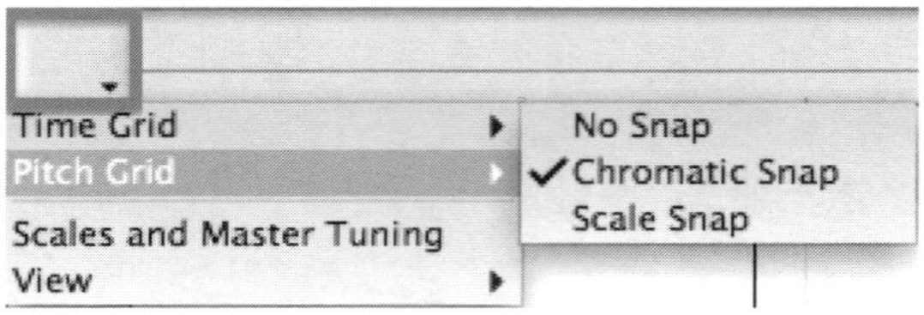

Figure 7-18

Choosing a Scale

If you select Scale Snap, Melodyne will detect the current scale but you can override that by enabling Scales and Master Tuning.

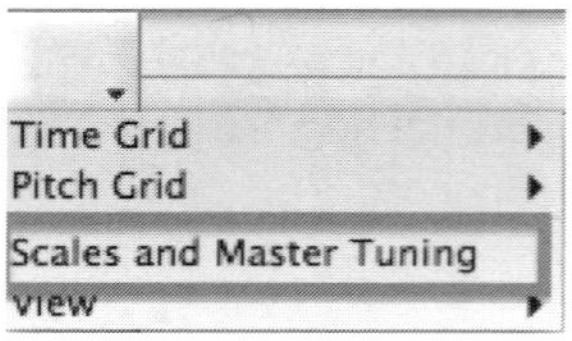

Figure 7-19

Then choose Open Scale from the scales drop-down list and choose from a wide variety of scales.

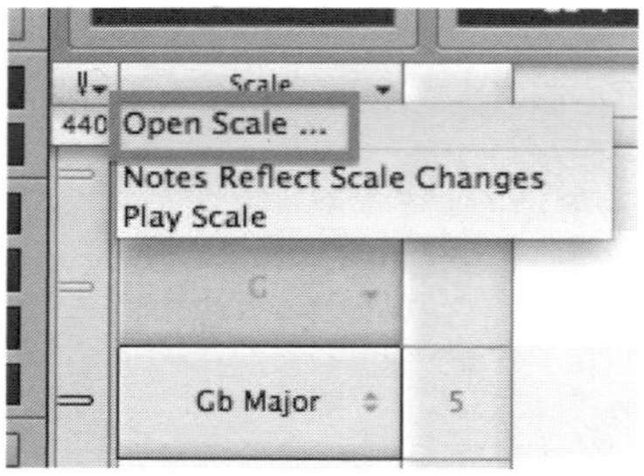

Figure 7-20

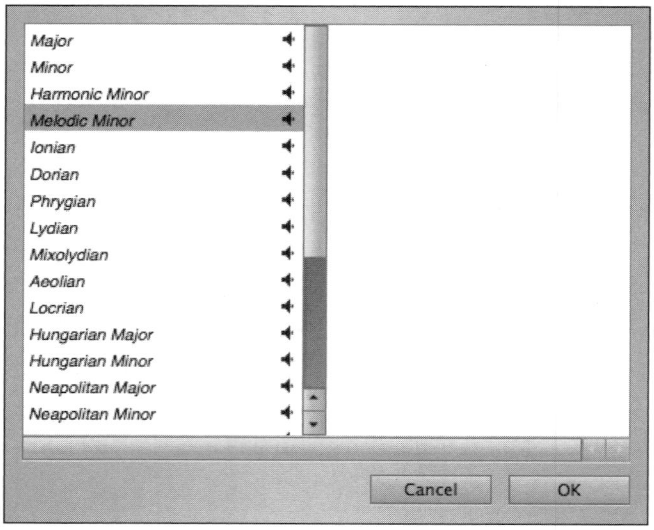

Figure 7-21

Adjusting Pitch

There are several ways to adjust the pitch of notes to correct tuning problems or change the arrangement. Let's take a look at them:

Double-click. To correct pitch to the selected scale, just double-click on a Blob with the Pitch tool, and it will be snapped to the nearest scale tone. If you select several Blobs, then double-click on one and they will all snap to pitch. Note: This works in Melodyne Editor but not Melodyne Essential.

Drag Vertically. Drag a Blob up or down with the Main tool, and it will snap based on your Pitch Grid settings. Set Pitch Grid to "No Snap" to adjust the pitch independent of the grid, or just hold down Opt / Alt to temporarily override snapping.

Correct Pitch Dialog Box

I usually prefer to work out pitch note by note, but if you are in a hurry, you can tune up the entire track using a simple dialog box with two sliders. Click on the Correct Pitch button on the right, then adjust the sliders until it sounds good!

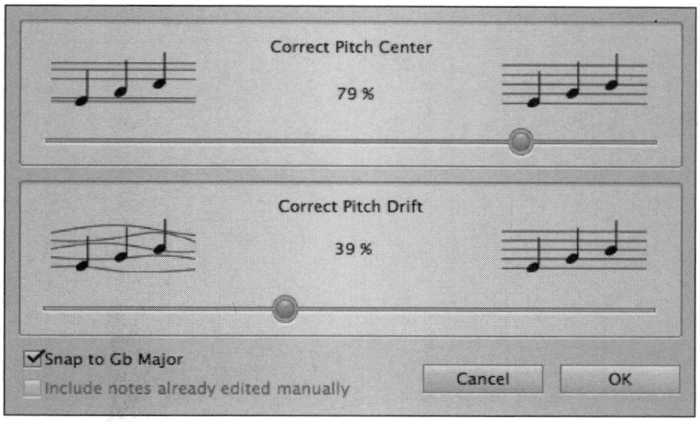

Figure 7-22

Time Snap

Melodyne is famous for correcting tuning, but it is no less capable when it comes to making time adjustments to audio. In Studio One, this gives you a great workflow for lead vocals. You can adjust pitch and timing with the same editing tool. Melodyne is an alternative to using Audio Bend for correcting timing on individual tracks.

Turn on Activate Grid from the drop-down menu in the upper right corner of the Melodyne Edit view or from the menu Edit > Time Grid.

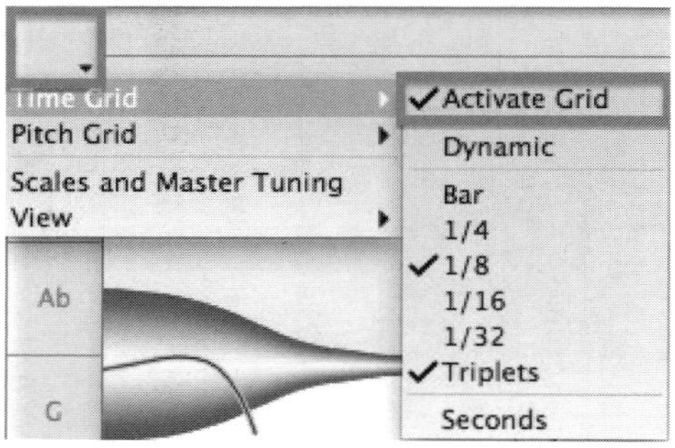

Figure 7-23

With Active Grid selected, you can choose from the musical time values on the same menu to define the grid increments. You can alternatively pick the Dynamic option to allow the grid to automatically adapt to the current zoom level. This works similarly to Studio One Adaptive snap. The grid and snap settings are independent of those in Studio One proper, so you will need to pick the appropriate settings here.

With the grid active, as you drag Blobs left and right they will snap to line up with the grid. You can override this while dragging by holding down Opt / Alt.

Tempo Detection

Melodyne does a great job of detecting the tempo of audio files. If you need to work with audio but don't know the tempo, just drag the file to a track and select Edit with Melodyne. Melodyne tempo detection kicks in automatically and shows the result in parenthesis right after host tempo. Once you know the tempo, you can set the file tempo in the Event properties.

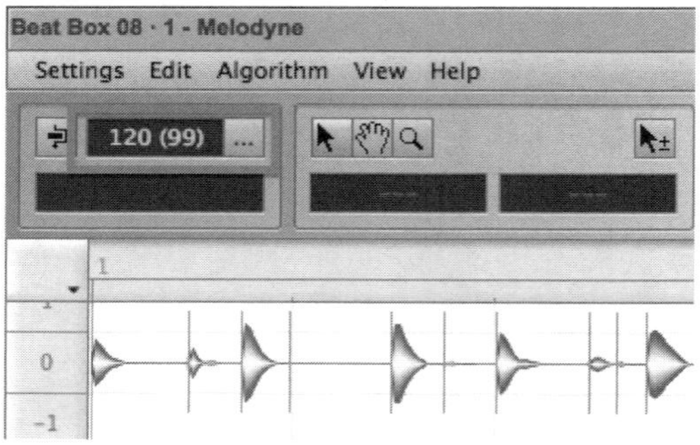

Figure 7-24

Quantize Time

You can use the Melodyne time grid to quantize audio in a very simple way. Select the Blobs for the notes you want to adjust or just press Cmd + A / Ctrl + A to select them all. Click on the Quantize Time button on the far right side of the Melodyne Edit view. From here you can pick a groove reference and adjust the slider. The more you slide to the right, the more the notes will align to the grid. Give it a try as an alternative to the Studio One native audio quantize and Audio Bend functions.

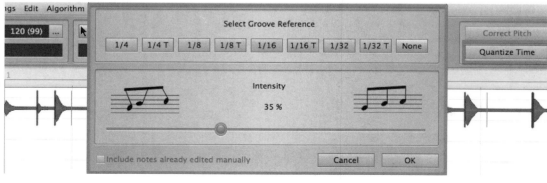

Figure 7-25

Chapter 8

INSTRUMENT PARTS

AND VIRTUAL INSTRUMENTS (MIDI)

In Studio One the word "MIDI" is used only when referencing external MIDI hardware. Since it is important to understand this chapter, here are the essential MIDI terms translated to Studio One lingo:

- MIDI track = Instrument Track
- MIDI clip = Instrument Part (a specific kind of Event)
- MIDI note = Note (or Note data)

About Instrument Parts

An Instrument Part is an event in the Arrange view that acts as a container for Note data. You can do many of the same editing tasks to the Instrument Part that you can do for Audio Events. The mouse tools work largely the same way, with a few exceptions.

Relative to Audio Events, there are a few things that you can't do with Instrument Parts. For example you can't edit the event volume graphically. There is no Volume box at the top center of Instrument Events. You can, however, edit the velocity percent in the Event Inspector or right-click on context menu for a similar effect.

Also, there are no Fade Flags, so you can't do graphic fades and crossfades. You can do this with other automation tools or by editing the Notes in the Editor. In addition, you can, easily bounce Instrument Parts with Cmd + B / Ctrl + B, which will let you use them as Audio Events along with the normal volume and fade tools.

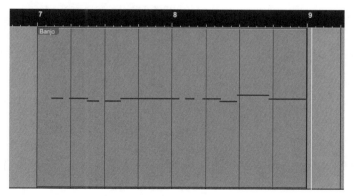

Figure 8-1

Editing Instrument Parts

The Range, Split, Erase, Paint, Mute, and Listen tools all work largely the same with Instrument Parts as for Audio Events. Keep in mind, an Instrument Part is a container event that appears in the Arrange view. When editing an Instrument Part, you are working with chunks of Notes rather than the individual Notes. Note editing happens in the Music Editor, and I will cover that shortly.

Here are the essential workflows for editing Instrument Parts:

Resize (Trim). Grab either the left or right edge of an Instrument Part and drag with the Arrow tool to resize the event.

Timestretch. Grab the right edge of an Instrument Part with the Arrow tool and drag left or right while holding down Opt / Alt to timestretch the part without altering the pitch.

Split. You can split Instrument Parts with the Split tool. You can also adjust the exact position of the split by dragging left or right at the slip point on the lower third of the event.

Duplicate. Press D to duplicate Instrument Parts just the way you would for Audio Events. Use the Duplicate Shared command (Shift + D) to create a reference to the same file. This allows edits to one event to be reflected in its copies.

Instrument Part Tips

You will find that working with Instrument Parts is very similar to working with Audio Parts. However, Instrument Parts have some unique features that allow you to take advantage of the underlying Note data. Here are some additional tips to use when working with Instrument Parts.

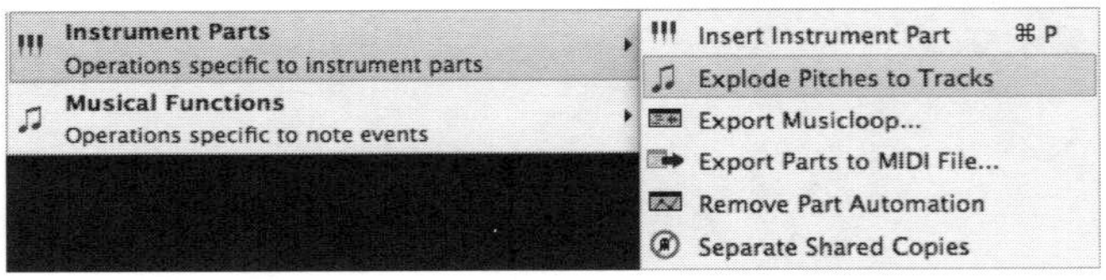

Figure 8-2

Exploding Pitches to Tracks

If you have a drum groove laid down as an Instrument Part but would rather mix it as if it were multitrack drums, then try Explode Pitches to Tracks (Event > Explode Pitches to Tracks). You will also find this on the right-click menu.

This will create a new Instrument Track for every note number used in the part. For drums this will effectively separate each part of the drum kit to its own track.

This will give you an entire set of events for the drums while muting the Instrument Parts. The key to getting clearly named tracks is to load or create a pitchmap for the drums. More on that shortly.

Figure 8-3

Tip: Track names for the exploded tracks are based on the original track name followed by the pitch name. If you want short track names, consider editing the original track and putting in a very short or even blank track name before running Explode Pitches to Tracks.

From here, convert the Instrument Parts to audio by bouncing using Cmd + B / Ctrl + B. Bouncing this way often results in stereo tracks for your drum parts. If you would rather see some of the drums as mono, change the track mode of those tracks to mono and bounce them again.

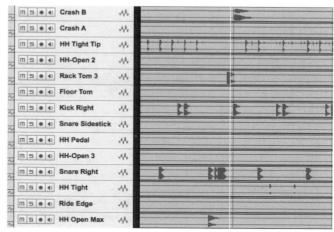

Figure 8-4

Creating an Empty Instrument Part

If you plan to draw in Notes or loop record drumbeats, it can help to start with a blank Instrument Part to give you a container to add something to. To do this, select the Paint tool (5) and swipe over the area where you would like to create the part.

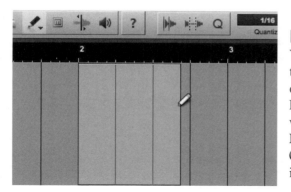

Figure 8-5

Exporting to MIDI

You can export an Instrument Part to a standard MIDI file (.mid) with drag-and-drop to the Studio One Browser. As you drag the part, you will see that you can select between Musicloop and MIDI File. Use Cmd / Ctrl to make the selection, then drop in the Browser.

Exporting to a Musicloop File

You can export to Musicloop files in the same way as MIDI Files. Drag an Instrument Part to the Browser and use Cmd / Ctrl to choose Musicloop. Musicloops contain the performance data as well as the virtual instrument setup and an audio preview. To see all the components of a Musicloop, right-click and select Show Package Contents.

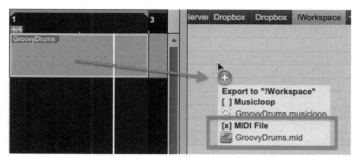

Figure 8-6

Music Editor

The main view for editing Notes in Studio One is the Music Editor. You get to it by double-clicking on any Instrument Part. It can also be opened and closed by pressing the F2 key. The Music Editor gives you access to the individual Notes in an Instrument Part. Notes are placed along the Timeline, referenced to a vertical piano keyboard on the left. In many other systems, this is called a "piano roll view" or a "MIDI editor."

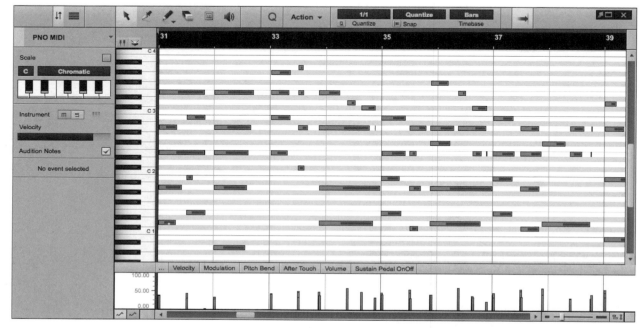

Figure 8-7

The Music Editor can be detached, moved to another screen, and expanded to full screen using the controls in the upper right corner. You can resize the Music Editor using the dividing bar between it and the Arrange view.

Figure 8-8

Figure 8-9

Selecting Which Tracks to Edit

If you have multiple Instrument Tracks, you can choose which Notes are shown here in several different ways. The first way is to use Link Track Selection. With this activated, when you select tracks in the Arrange view, the Notes become visible in the Music Editor.

You can also choose any available Instrument Track with the track selector drop-down list at the top of the properties area. This is a very convenient way to switch between tracks without needing to go back to the Arrange view.

For more detailed control over what you are editing, use the Track List. This works similarly to the Track List in Arrange view. It reveals a list of Instrument Tracks in the Song. The dot at the beginning of each row is used to show or hide that track in the Editor. Click on the pencil at the end of the row to enable or disable it for editing. The Track List allows you to edit one or more tracks at the same time. If you want to focus on just one of them, you can disable all the others. You can open the Track List as needed or close it to save screen space.

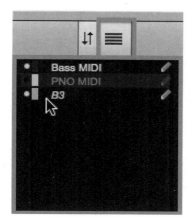

Figure 8-10

Music Editor Toolbar

The Toolbar and mouse tools are basically the same as what we have already covered for editing Events. In this context, however, they are specialized for editing Notes.

Figure 8-11

> **Tip:** Check out Info view to discover important modifiers for the mouse tools. This is an essential resource when working in the Music Editor.

Arrow Tool. Use the Arrow tool to move Notes. Up and down will change the pitch. You can hear the Note as it snaps into position if Audition Notes is turned on.

Drag left or right to move the Note forward or backward in time. If Snap is on, it will snap to the nearest grid position. Drag the left or right edge of the Note to trim the length. Duplicate a Note by pressing D, just like with event editing. The standard commands of cut, copy, and paste all work as well.

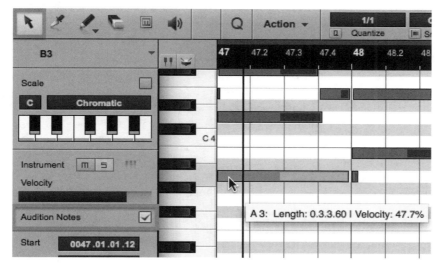

Figure 8-12

Split Tool. Click on a Note with the Split tool to split it into two. Check out the Info view for some modifiers. Pressing Cmd / Ctrl changes the Split tool to the Arrow tool temporarily. As you click, hold down Opt / Alt to split the Note and the containing Event.

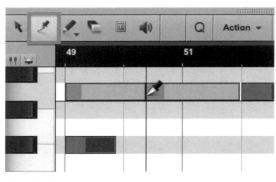

Figure 8-13

Paint Tool. The Paint tool is very powerful for Note editing. Click to add Notes and drag right to paint in the length. Continue dragging up and down to set the velocity. The Paint tool is influenced by the snap settings as well as the scale (vertical snap) setting, which we will talk about shortly.

Use the Paint tool to trim the length by just dragging the right or left edge of the Note. This works exactly like the Arrow tool for this purpose.

Hold down Opt / Alt and drag up and down on a Note or selection of Notes to adjust the velocity. Use this command to edit the velocity of an existing Note. Velocity is shown on the Note as a two-tone color code. You can also watch the percentage change next to the Velocity tool.

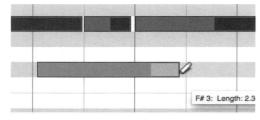

Figure 8-14

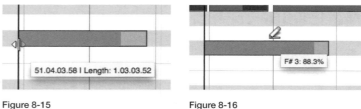

Figure 8-15

Figure 8-16

Figure 8-17

Eraser Tool. Click on a Note with the Eraser tool to delete it. You can also swipe over a group of Notes to take them out.

Mute Tool. Click with the Mute tool to mute Notes without removing them. They appear ghosted and won't play.

Listen Tool. The Listen tool starts playback wherever you click. It plays only the audio from the track you click on. That saves you a lot of time, because there's a lot less soloing that you have to do with this tool.

Actions

The Music Editor Toolbar includes a drop-down list of actions. For any of these actions, select one or more Notes, then choose the action from the list. Some of the actions have keyboard shortcuts preassigned, but you can assign your own shortcut to actions you use often.

Most of the actions will start with a dialog box of options. For example, select some Notes and choose Stretch. You see additional options for Double Tempo, Half Tempo, or Free where you can set a multiplier. All of these are useful. I frequently use the Stretch, Transpose, Delete Double Notes, and Delete Short Notes actions.

Split at Grid is another useful action. For example, create a one bar hi-hat and set the grid to eighth notes and choose Split at Grid. That chops the single hi-hat Note into an eighth-note pattern.

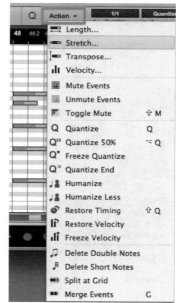

Figure 8-18

Figure 8-19

Auto Scroll

Enable Auto Scroll (F) to keep the playback cursor onscreen. With Auto Scroll on, when the cursor gets to the right edge of the screen, the view will update to follow the cursor. It can be helpful to leave this off when editing in a loop to prevent whatever you are focused on from leaving the view.

Figure 8-20

Pitch Names

The keyboard to the left of the Music Editor can be replaced with a Pitch Names view by clicking on the Drum icon tab. In other systems this might be called a "drum map." The point is to assign friendly names to each scale tone in situations when you aren't really playing normal keyboard notes.

This is most useful when working with drums, because you can see a row for each drum instrument. In addition, the Explode Pitches to Tracks function will use the pitch names as part of the track name, so it really helps to have the pitches set correctly.

Figure 8-21

Use the Edit icon to edit the pitch names and save or load preset maps.

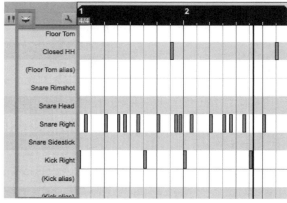

Figure 8-22

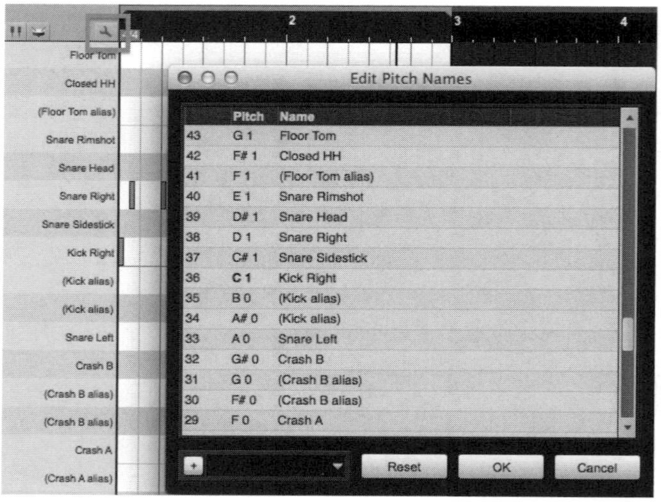

Figure 8-23

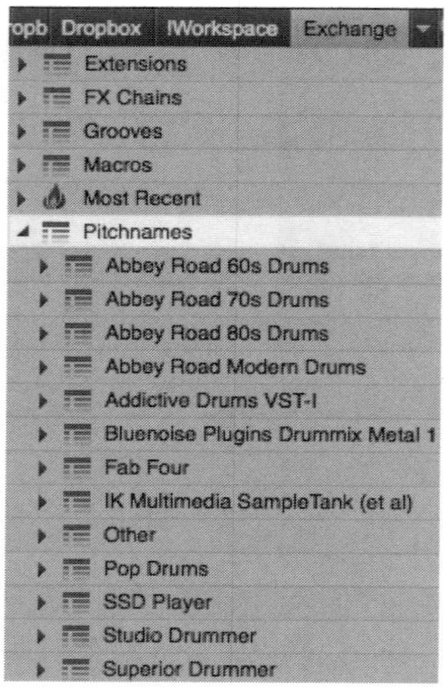

Figure 8-24

Use PreSonus Exchange in the Browser to find and load pitchmaps for many popular drum instruments created by other users.

Track and Note Properties

You can set additional Track and Note properties on the left side of the Music Editor. Let's take a look at what each of these options does:

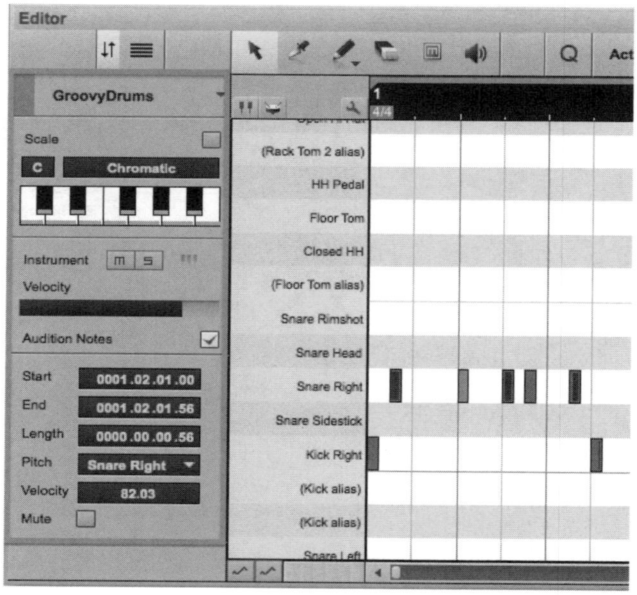

Figure 8-25

Figure 8-26

Track Select. Use this drop-down list to choose which track to edit.

Scale Snap (Vertical Snap). Use this to turn Scale snap on or off and set the key and scale using the scale properties. Scale snapping applies to new Notes added with the Paint tool, Notes moved with the Arrow tool, and Notes copied with the Arrow tool. If you wanted to quickly harmonize a line in one of your melodies, you can turn this on, select a few Notes, and then do an Opt / Alt drag to instantly create a parallel harmony.

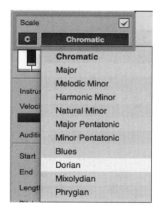

Figure 8-27

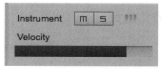

Figure 8-28

Track Controls. This properties area includes track Mute and Solo controls for your convenience. Click on the Instrument icon to open the window for the virtual instrument. The Velocity slider sets the initial velocity for Notes you draw in with the Paint tool.

Audition Notes. With Audition Notes turned on, Notes will play back when they are clicked, moved, or drawn.

Note Properties. This section shows all the properties for individual Notes. Select a Note and you can see its start, end, length, pitch, and velocity values. You can also change any of the values. I often edit the pitch and Note properties this way. I find it easy to switch octaves by just editing C2 to C3 for example. You can select a pitch from the list or double-click on the Pitch property and just type it in.

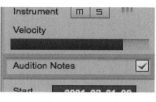

Figure 8-29

Editing Controller Values

You can edit controller data for each Note in one of two controller views at the bottom of the Music Editor. Click on one of the four standard controls: Velocity, Modulation, Pitch Bend, or After Touch. This will bring the associated controllers into view.

Figure 8-30

Figure 8-31

You can add any other controller by clicking on the Add button and selecting from the Automation dialog box.

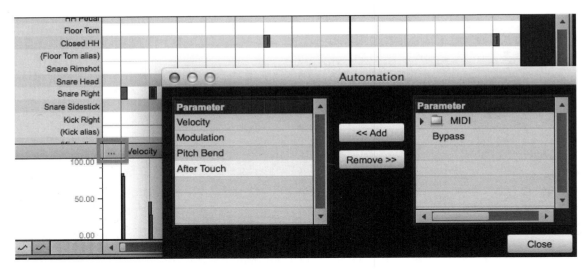

Figure 8-32

Edit the controller value by adjusting the height of the stalk with the Arrow tool or the Paint tool. For stacked Notes, select the Note you want to modify first, and then only that controller will be shown. This style of controller editing is pretty common with MIDI editors, so this should seem familiar.

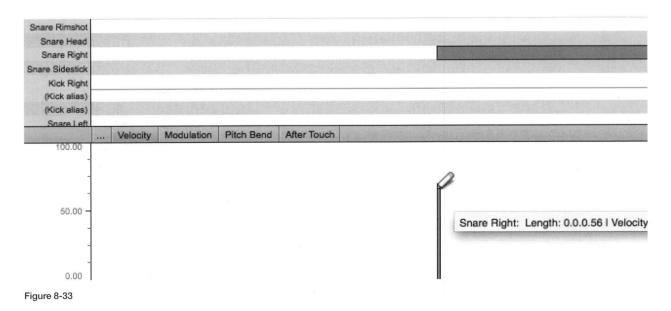

Figure 8-33

You can have both controller views open at the same time and set to different controllers.

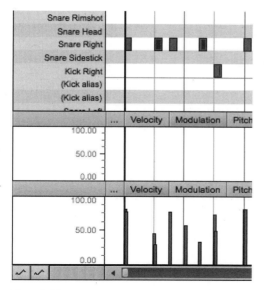

Figure 8-34

You can make controller edits on a selection of Notes at the same time. To do this, select all the Notes you want to edit and adjust the velocity of one of them. The controller stalks will all move together proportionally.

> **Tip:** You can select a row of Notes by holding down Cmd / Ctrl and clicking on the piano key or drum for the corresponding note. The entire row will be selected. Now you can adjust velocity or other parameters together. This is really valuable for editing drum parts!

Quantizing Notes

If you are coming from a background of working with many other DAWs, you would call this section "Quantizing MIDI." MIDI notes are just called Notes in Studio One, so I will stick with that terminology. The Quantize panel that I introduced for quantizing audio is also use for quantizing Notes, but there are additional actions available in both the Music Editor and the Arrange view.

Quantize Actions

In Arrange view, you quantize by selecting one or more Instrument Parts (MIDI clip) then choosing a quantize action from the right-click menu under Musical Functions. In Arrange view, quantizing actions affect all of the Notes contained in the Instrument Part.

In the Music Editor quantize functions appear in the Action drop-down menu on the Toolbar. Quantizing in the Music Editor only affects the current selection of Notes. For example, if you want to humanize a programmed hi-hat part while leaving all the other drums untouched, you would select all the hi-hat Notes and then choose Humanize from the Action drop-down menu.

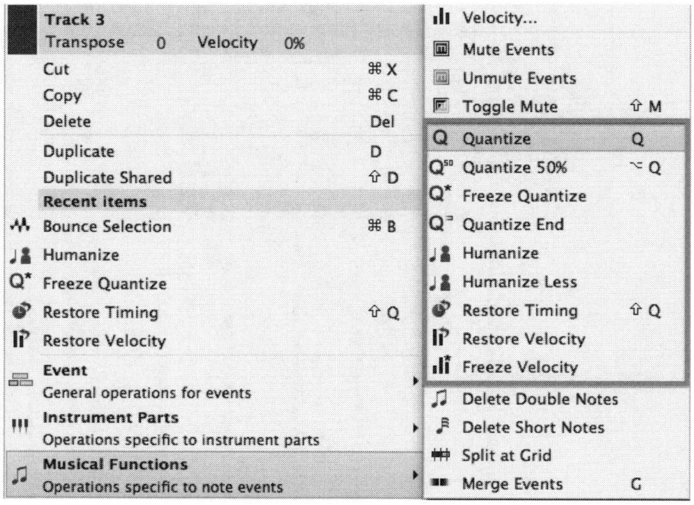

Figure 8-35

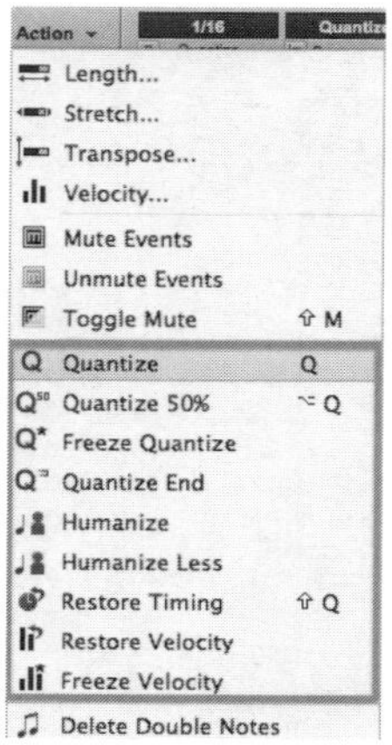

Quantize. To quantize, select the Quantize grid, select the Notes you want to quantize, and hit Q. Try a different quantize setting and hit Q again. You can also find Quantize as an option in the Action drop-down menu.

Quantize 50%. Use Opt + Q / Alt + Q to quantize with start strength set to 50%. This is a really good way to tighten up a part without taking all groove out.

Freeze Quantize. Select Freeze Quantize from the Action list to lock in your quantize setting. Now if you make additional quantize adjustments, you can get back to this value using Restore Timing from the Action list.

Quantize End. Using Quantize End from the Action list is a quick way to adjust the Note length to the nearest grid increment. You can adjust the strength of the Quantize End action by adjusting the End parameter in the Quantize panel.

Humanize. This action adds small timing variations and velocity variations to make a part less mechanical. This can improve the groove and feel of a programmed part, compared with something that is perfectly quantized.

Figure 8-36

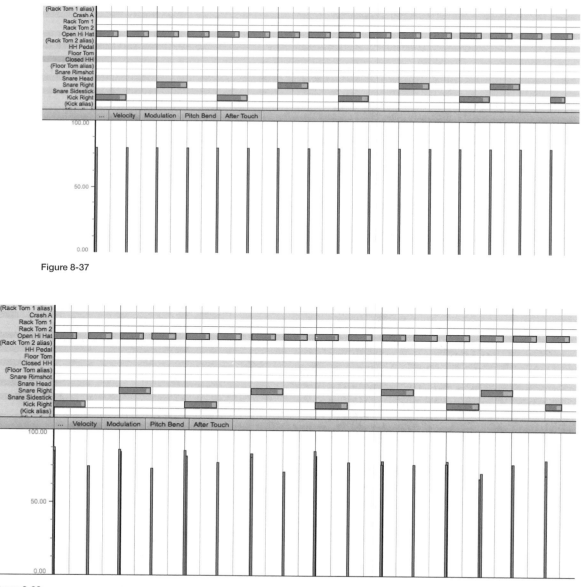

Figure 8-37

Figure 8-38

Humanize Less. Humanize Less does the same thing as Humanize, just with less intensity.

Restore Timing. If you have been playing with quantizing and want to reset the Notes to their original timing, use Restore Timing (Shift + Q). This will put the timing back either to where you were when you started applying quantizing or where you were the last time you used Freeze Quantize.

Restore Velocity. Restore Velocity puts your velocity back to where it was when you started editing the velocity or where you were the last time you used Freeze Velocity.

Freeze Velocity. This locks in your velocity edits. After using Freeze Velocity, Restore Velocity will take you back to this point in time.

Auto Quantize

If you want to try a lot of different quantize settings, turn on Auto Quantize. As you make changes to the setup, the results are reflected in the Notes immediately. This is great way to experiment with all the options in the Quantize panel. You can always clear your experiments using Restore Timing.

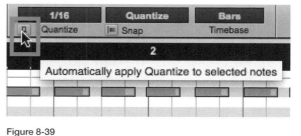

Figure 8-39

Note: Auto Quantize is not the same thing as Input Quantize (Options > Input Quantize). Input Quantize will quantize your performance as you play or record in Studio One.

Quantize Panel

For more control over quantize, open the Quantize panel. This gives you more options for setting up the Quantize grid based on musical functions. It also provides more options for setting quantize strength.

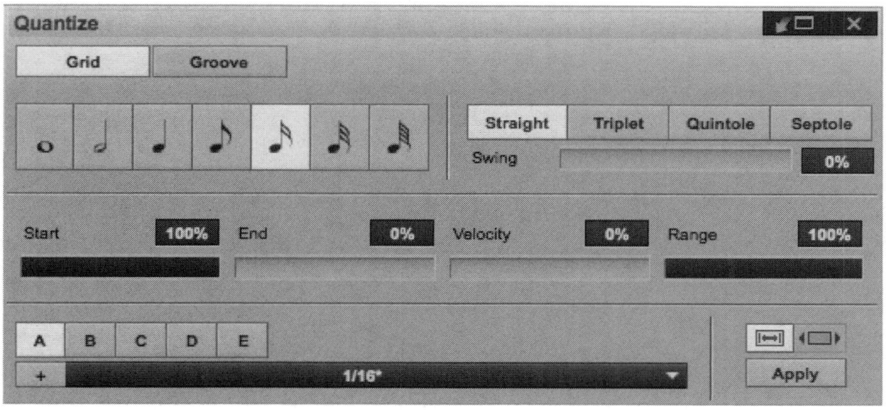

Figure 8-40

There are four strength options for quantizing Notes available in the Quantize panel. Here are the details on what they do:

Figure 8-41

Start. Start is essentially quantize strength. It makes the beginning of the Note snap to the nearest grid increment. If you have Auto Quantize turned on, you will see the result immediately after making a change.

End. The End value sets the strength of the quantizing for the Quantize End action. Notes will be stretched toward the nearest grid increment based on how high this is set.

Velocity. The Velocity value allows you to scale the Velocity parameter as you quantize. If you turn off all the other parameters and turn Auto Quantize on, you can adjust the velocity scaling independently in real time during playback.

Range. Range defines a zone near grid lines that are active for quantizing. If Notes fall outside of the range, they don't get quantized at all. With Range set to 100%, all Notes are quantized. This is useful for retaining the groove of the Notes. It's also useful if you're quantizing something that's got a lot of busy fills.

Included Virtual Instruments

You can use almost any popular third-party virtual instruments in Studio One with your Instrument Tracks. PreSonus provides four excellent built-in instruments. I don't have room in this book to get into detail on these, but here is short description of each one:

SampleOne. SampleOne is a sampler-type instrument. You can drag audio files directly from the Arrange view or the Browser to SampleOne, and the sample gets mapped across the keyboard. If you drag in an Audio Part, the slices get mapped to different keys. Also, if you right-click on an Audio Loop or REX file in the Browser, you can send it to SampleOne with the slices mapped across the keyboard.

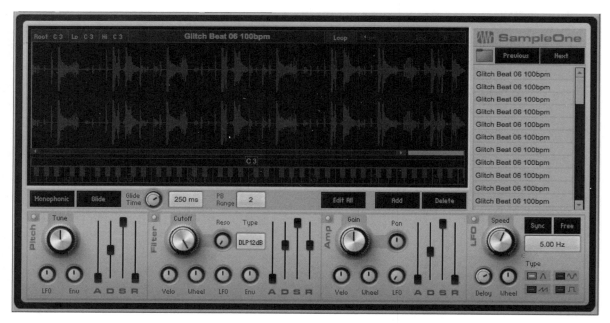

Figure 8-42

Presence. Presence is a general-purpose sample-playback-style instrument, with a wide range of presets covering the most essential sounds. Presence sounds range from very nice grand pianos to bass guitar to drum kits. Presence features straightforward filter and modulation controls on the main screen, with a second view dedicated to an excellent range off effects.

Figure 8-43

Mojito. Mojito is inspired by the great monophonic synths of the '70s, and can help you get vintage Moog-style leads, basses, or modern wobble tones. Editing is very simple, with only a single view of knobs and properties. It has some interesting features like the ability to morph between sawtooth and square waves. Since Studio One 2, Mojito has gained a very useful suboscillator control to fatten out any sound.

Figure 8-44

Impact. Impact is a drum instrument configured as a 4 × 4 matrix of pads. Each pad can have multiple samples that can be mapped to different velocity ranges. In addition each sample uses several sound-shaping tools and envelopes. As a result Impact can be used as a realistic drum sound source for recording or a sound-design tool for percussion or even remixing. Impact supports multiple console channels. Each pad can be assigned to any available channel.

Figure 8-45

PART III: STUDIO ONE PROFESSIONAL MIXING

Chapter 9
THE STUDIO ONE CONSOLE

The Console view is the virtual mixer in Studio One. Most DAWs have a similar view, so in concept it should feel familiar. In Studio One, Audio Tracks and channels have a one-to-one correspondence. For every Audio Track you will find a matching console channel.

For instruments it works a bit differently. A virtual instrument (VI) is loaded in the Instrument panel in the Console and can have several output channels. Several Instrument Tracks can be assigned to a single instance of a VI. Arrange view Instrument Tracks are assigned to VIs in the Console view. Once you get that straight, the Console view should feel right at home!

Open the Console view at any time by hitting F3 on the keyboard. F3 toggles the Console open and closed. Another way is to click on the Mix button in the lower right corner of Studio One. Detach the Console to a floating window using the controls in the upper right corner. From here you can resize it, move it to a second monitor, or make it full screen.

Figure 9-1

Console View Options and Panels

Figure 9-2

The left side of the Console view has a series of vertical buttons that allow you to hide or show features of the Console. These need a little explanation:

1. **Small or Large Console.** Choose between the Small or Large Console mode. The Large view makes Insert bins and Sends visible on all the channels. The Small view is more compact so the Inserts and Sends are hidden, but you can open them using the expand arrow channel by channel.

2. **Narrow or Normal Console.** If you want to see more channels onscreen at the same time, you can switch to the Narrow Console mode. This can help you get the full mix onscreen, even with a modest-size monitor. Narrow mode retains full metering, so you can get a nice overview of the whole song.

3. **Inputs.** Click to show channels for all available inputs. These are the actual hardware inputs that you defined in Song Setup. This is a quick way to get an overview of your recording levels. You can even put inserts directly on the input channels. Then, anything that you record through those effects will actually get printed to the track as you record. This is a great feature of Studio One. I do this with guitar amp simulators if I just want to commit to the sound up-front.

4. **Outputs.** This feature allows you to show or hide the output channels. It gives you a direct view of the signal to those outputs. This is most helpful if you have additional outputs defined for headphone cue mixes. You might also want to see these if you are mixing through an external mixer or summing device.

5. **Trash.** This option allows you to restore effects and instruments you have removed from the Song with their previous settings. You can even drag effects or instruments from the Trash to the Arrange view. This way you can create new tracks or apply the setup to other tracks.

6. **External.** This opens a list of all external hardware that has been connected. This includes keyboards, controllers, and instruments.

7. **Instruments.** This option reveals all instances of virtual instruments. You can add, remove, or silence instruments here. Instruments that currently have no track assignment appear in gray lettering.

8. **Banks.** The Banks panel is a list of every channel in the Console view. It does for console channels what the Track List does for tracks. Next, we will go into a bit more detail on the Banks panel.

Banks Panel

The Banks panel has two tabs: Screen and Remote. Most of the time you can leave this set to Screen, which is the setup for the onscreen view of the Console. Use the list of channels to quickly hide and show channels in the Console view. This allows you to focus on the channels you're working with. You can toggle channel displays on and off by clicking on them in the Banks list. Swipe over a series of channels to hide them in one pass.

The four filters along the bottom of the Banks panel are Tracks, Instruments, FX, and Buses. These allow you to quickly hide any of these four

Figure 9-3

classes of channels. Keep in mind that this is for the view of the Console only—none of this has any effect on sound.

> **Tip:** If you enable Link Track List / Console in the Arrange view Track List, whatever you hide or show in Banks will also hide or show the corresponding tracks.

The Banks view includes a preset system that lets you save snapshots and quickly return to your favorite mix views. For example, I often create a setup of all my drum channels. Then I show only drums when I focus on that. Another setup shows all channels along with the drum Bus Channel while leaving all the separate drum channels hidden.

Banks Panel Remote Tab

The Remote tab gives you a full second setup for the Console view. If you have an external fader device configured, this is the view of the Console that the fader bank will see. For example, if you have external control surface with eight faders, you can assign which faders will be active on the Remote tab of the Banks panel.

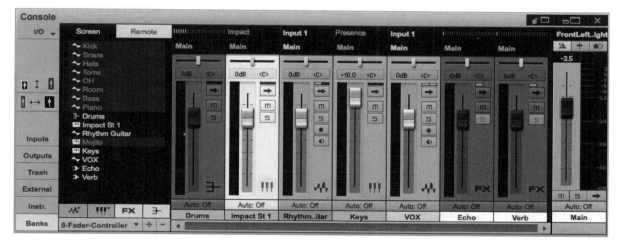

Figure 9-4

Audio Channel Strips

Every time you add an Audio Track to the Arrange view, you also add a corresponding channel to the mixer in Console view. All the other kinds of channels share most of the same features, so let's take a look at a typical audio channel in more detail:

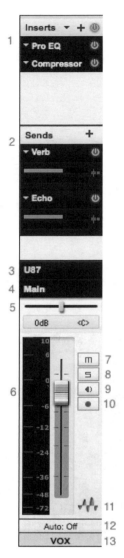

Figure 9-5

1. **Inserts Bin.** Each channel has an Inserts bin. (Note: The PreSonus Studio One 2 Reference Manual calls bins like this "device racks," but that's a little wordy for our purposes here.) Drag-and-drop effects from the Browser or click on the Add Effect button. You can drag effects to reorder them. I will be going over this section in detail a bit later.

2. **Sends Bin.** You can add send objects to the Sends section of each channel. You can send to Bus Channels, FX Channels, or the sidechain inputs of effects. I will cover those scenarios coming up.

3. **Input Selection.** Click to select from any available input. This is typically the actual hardware input used for recording. The names are configured in Song Setup. This is repeated from the track. If you change the input here, it will change on the track as well.

4. **Output Selection.** Use this option to set the output destination. Usually the output will be set to the Main Output, but it can be routed to any available Bus Channel or FX Channels. You can send either to the master out or to individual buses or effects from this point. You can also send outputs to sidechain inputs of effects. However, Sends are usually used for sidechain setups.

5. **Panner.** The Panner control positions mono signals anywhere between the left and right speakers. For stereo signals the Panner acts as a balance control. For example, if you pan hard left, you hear only the left side. To recenter pan, click while holding down Cmd / Ctrl.

> **Tip:** For full-pan position control over stereo signals, check out the Dual Pan effect. This gives you separate pan knobs for left and right.

6. **Fader.** Adjust the channel fader by dragging up and down or left and right. Hold down Shift as you drag for finer adjustment. Holding down Cmd / Ctrl while clicking will reset the fader back to 0 dB. Notice the numeric setting above the fader. Double-click on it to type in a fader value between –infinity and +10 dB.

7. **Mute.** This option mutes the channel. If the channel is grouped, the group will be muted. Shift-click on the Mute button to mute an individual track within a group.

8. **Solo.** Pressing Shift-click enables Save Solo mode. The Solo button turns light green and the track is not soloed, but when you solo any other track this track will automatically be soloed, too. FX Channels are in Save Solo mode by default, so you can hear effects when soloing tracks. I use it to keep the drum track going as I solo other instruments.

9. **Input Monitor.** Click to hear the live input signal processed through this channel. Enabling this option is essential when using guitar amp simulators like Ampire.

10. **Record Enable.** Works just like on the track. This needs to be on in order to record audio to this track.

11. **Channel Icon.** The particular icon indicates which kind of track you are looking at: Audio, Instrument, Bus, or FX. For Instrument Channels, clicking on the icon will bring up the window for the instrument.

12. **Automation.** This allows you to set the automation mode for the channel to Off, Read, Touch, Latch, or Write. I will cover this in detail in the section about automation.

13. **Channel Color and Name.** Click on the color block and choose the color. Double-click to edit the channel name. For Audio Tracks, the color and name will also change in the Arrange view if you change them here.

Cue Mix Faders

If you configure extra outputs with the Cue option in Song Setup, a cue mix fader section will appear below the Sends bin. There will be as many as you have cue outputs configured. We went over this setup in more detail in the recording section of this book.

Figure 9-6

Expanding Channels

When using the Small view of the mixer, the Inserts and Sends bins are hidden to by default. If you click on the expand arrow, the Inserts and Sends open to the right of channel. This gives you full access to all channel functions even when the Console is small. If you have additional outputs configured as cue mixes, then the cue mix faders will appear as well.

The two blue indicators that look like LEDs above the expand arrow indicate if there is anything in the Inserts or Sends bins. The left is for the Inserts and the right is for the Sends. It is a nice visual cue to use when the expanded view is closed.

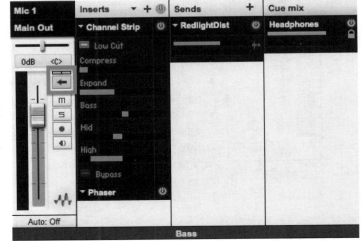

Figure 9-7

Channel Groups

To group a series of channels so the faders all work together, Shift-select a range of channels and pick Group Selected Tracks from the right-click menu or hit Cmd + G / Ctrl + G.

Once they're grouped, moving one fader will move the others proportionally. The output selection, mute, solo, record, monitor, automation mode, and track color are all synchronized. The Inserts, Sends, Input, and Panner continue to operate independently. For Audio Tracks, grouping the channels also groups the corresponding tracks for editing.

Figure 9-8

To temporarily override the group for a channel, hold down Opt / Alt while moving the fader or control.

To get rid of a group, choose Dissolve Group from the right-click menu or use the keyboard shortcut Shift + Cmd + G / Shift + Ctrl + G.

Tip: To temporarily group faders, simply Shift-select a range of channels and they will move together proportionally.

Bus Channels

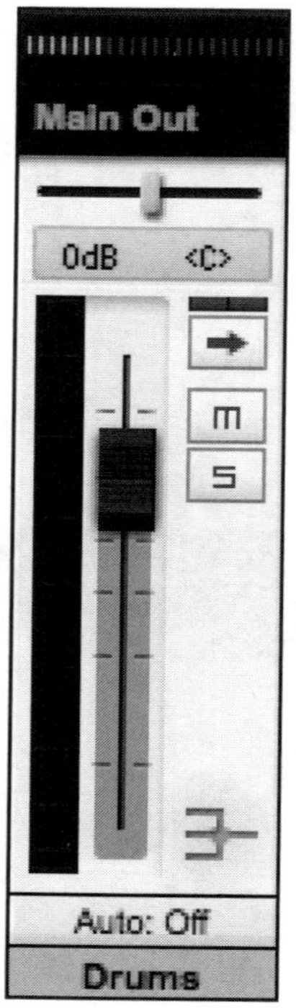

A Bus Channel is similar in concept to an auxiliary input on other systems. In operation, a Bus Channel is similar to an audio channel, but there is no associated Arrange view track. You can't record to a Bus Channel, but you can route other channels to them. Bus Channels include Mute and Solo buttons but lack Record and Monitor buttons.

This gives you an intermediate level of faders and effect inserts to use on groups of tracks. A common use is to route all your drum channels into a drum bus. This gives you a single fader to control the drum level for the mix. It also gives you a way to add compression or EQ to the entire kit.

You can also run a Bus Channel into another bus. This allows you to create a submix within a submix. For example, you may wish to route three snare channels to a single bus, then route that to the drum bus.

There are many ways to create a Bus Channel:

- Right-click on some blank space in the mixer and choose Add Bus Channel.
- Use the I/O drop-down menu at the left of the Console.
- Shift-select a range of channels, then choose Add Bus for Selected Channels from the right-click menu.
- You can create a Bus Channel for the contents of a Folder Track by clicking on the Bus property and selecting Add Bus for Selected Channels.

Bus Channels have Inserts and Sends just like audio channels. You can't pick the input, because inputs to buses are assigned at the source. There is a graphic above the fader on Bus Channels that indicates how many sources feed the channel (Figure 9-10). If you click on this graphic, you can see and select any of the source channels.

Figure 9-9

Figure 9-10

FX Channels

FX Channels are created whenever you drag an effect to a send on a channel. Another way to create an FX Channel is to right-click on blank space in the mixer and select Create FX Channel.

FX Channels are intended to be used for master effects when mixing. Using them is also a great way to add parallel compression to tracks. Assign Sends to FX Channels from the Sends bin Plus icon of any channel or by just dragging an effect from the Browser to a Send. FX Channels are in Save Solo mode by default, so the FX Channel will be heard when associated channels are soloed.

The Difference Between FX Channels and Bus Channels

FX and Bus Channels are very similar and differ primarily in their intention. Typically, your mix will be easier to set up and understand if you use FX for master effects and buses for submixes, as intended. Here are the specific differences between the two:

- Bus Channels have Sends bins; FX Channels don't.
- FX Channels are in Save Solo mode by default.
- FX Channels are created when you drag an effect to a send or track.
- Bus Channels and FX Channels have separate filters on the Banks panel.

Main Out

The Main Out is a dedicated Bus Channel. Since it is the last thing in the signal flow, it doesn't have a Sends bin. Instead, there is a Post Effects bin. This would typically be used for a final limiter or dithering plug-in. The Main Out also includes a metronome on/off and level. There is also a Mono/Stereo mode button. Mute and Solo

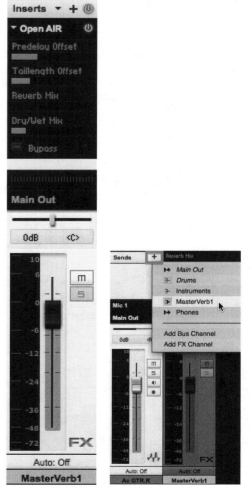

Figure 9-11   Figure 9-12

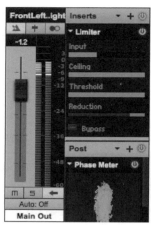

Figure 9-13

are below the fader, and the meter is a bit bigger than on a typical Bus Channel. The channel name does not need to be Main Out. You can edit the name with a double-click or change it in Song Setup (Song > Song Setup > Audio I/O Setup). Click-and-hold to change the Main Out color.

Figure 9-14

Figure 9-15

The Main Out also features a Post bin. This is for applying effects post fader. The most common use of this would be to apply a dithering plug-in such as Waves L2 when reducing bit depth. If you use the Post bin for this, make sure to disable automatic dithering in Options. It is also common to put a metering plug-in and other analysis plug-ins in the Post bin.

Instrument Channels

Instrument Channels function as outputs for virtual instruments (VIs). They feature Inserts and Sends bins, output selection, as well as Fader, Panner, Mute, and Solo controls. You don't specifically create Instrument Channels; they are added to the mixer automatically when you load a VI instance.

The input selection is fixed to the corresponding virtual instrument instance. If you click on the Input property or the Track Type icon, the window for the virtual instrument will load.

The relationship between Instrument Tracks (Arrange view) and virtual Instrument Channels (Console view) is different from many DAWs, which makes it a point of confusion for people who are new to Studio One. An Instrument Track and a virtual Instrument Channel don't always have a one-to-one relationship.

Note data (MIDI, essentially) lives on Instrument Tracks, while the virtual instrument instances live in the Console. An Instrument Track routes to a virtual instrument (VI) instance, and that is what connects these two concepts together. If you drag a virtual instrument from the Browser to the Arrange view, Studio One creates an Instrument Track, an instance of the VI, an Instrument Channel, and configures the routing. This may make it seem like the track contains the VI, which is not the case. Drag-and-drop is a workflow shortcut but does not reveal the underlying architecture.

An advantage to this approach is that it allows you to easily route an Instrument Track to different VIs or route multiple tracks to the same VI. This is very useful for programmed drums, among others.

Since VIs can have multiple outputs, Studio One allows you to turn them on and off as console channels. Open the Instrument panel, select a VI instance, and select Expand with the drop-down or context menu.

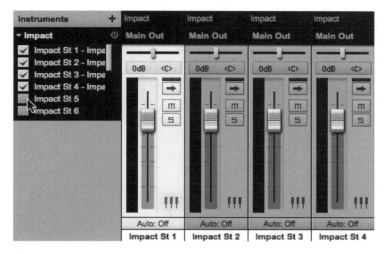

Figure 9-16

Disable or enable any of the available outputs. For each enabled output, you get an Instrument Channel in the Console. Instrument Channels have features similar to Bus Channels. The input is fixed to the associated VI, and the Track icon is set to the Instrument Channel type. Click on the Track icon to open the window for the assigned VI.

Navigating Console Channels

With large track counts, locating a specific channel can be a challenge. Studio One has some features to help with that. To find an Instrument or Audio Track, select Show in Console from the right-click menu. Studio One will select the corresponding channel and expand it if the mixer is in the Small mode. Instrument Tracks have a drop-down arrow in the upper right. You can find Show in Console there, as well.

Figure 9-17

Tip: You can move the channel selection backward and forward in the Console view with the Open Bracket ([) and Close Bracket (]) keys.

Chapter 10
WORKING WITH EFFECTS

It's easy to apply effects in Studio One using drag-and-drop: simply locate the plug-in effect you want to use in the Browser, and drag it to a channel. The effect loads into the Inserts area of the channel, and the plug-in window pops open for immediate tweaking.

When you drop an effect on the send area of a channel, Studio One automatically creates an FX Channel, loads the plug-in, and creates a send fader on the channel.

If you drop an effect on a track in the Arrange view, it loads into the Inserts area of the corresponding channel. This works for both Instrument and Audio Tracks. Drag-and-drop also can change the order of plug-ins, save FX chains, or copy effects track to track.

Note: The words "effect," "FX," and "plug-in" are used interchangeably in this section.

Supported Plug-Ins

Studio One supports VST and VST3 plug-ins on both Mac and Windows. If Studio One is running in 64-bit mode, it requires 64-bit plug-ins. Mac users can also use AU plug-ins.

There isn't any native support for adapting 32-bit plug-ins for use with the 64-bit version of Studio One. Some users report good results with third-party bit-bridging applications. Honestly, I don't like these solutions because they tend to compromise stability. My recommendation is that if you need to run 32-bit plug-ins, you should run Studio One in 32-bit mode.

Browsing Effects

Before you can drag an effect to a channel, you need to find it. If your system is like mine, you have hundreds of plug-ins available to choose from. The Studio One Browser has some convenient tools to help you find the right effect.

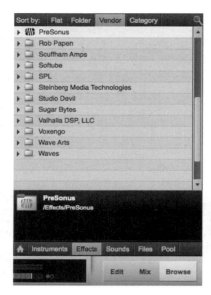

Figure 10-1

Press F7 to open the Browser with the Effects tab selected. Note the additional tabs along the top: Flat, Folder, Vendor, and Category. These give you different ways to view all available effects. Personally, I use the Vendor sort order most.

The Category sort order is also very useful. It organizes PreSonus effects by class: analysis, delay, mixing, reverb, and so on. It organizes third-party plug-ins by technology: AudioUnit, VST2, and VST3.

The real power here is in the search tool. Click on the Magnifying Glass icon to the upper right or press Cmd + F / Ctrl + F to open the search bar. Typing in a few characters of the plug-in name should be enough to find the effect you want.

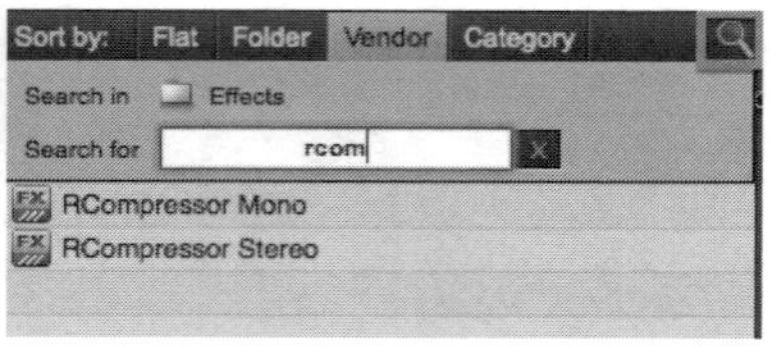

Figure 10-2

Once you find it, you can drag it into the channel. If it is a built-in effect, you can expand it with the triangle to the left to reveal the preset options. Drag one of these presets directly to a channel to load the effect with predetermined settings.

Most third-party effects have their own preset system. You can also save your own presets from the Studio One Effect window (rather than the effect's native system). Presets stored this way will appear in the Studio One Browser making it really fast to load the preset in the future using drag-and-drop.

Figure 10-3

Effect Inserts Bins

Effects run in the Inserts bin of channels. Every type of channel has an Inserts bin. Output channels like the Main Out have an additional "Post" bin that runs plug-ins after the fader.

The PreSonus Studio One 2 Reference Manual calls the Inserts bin the Inserts Device Rack, but I use the shorter "Inserts bin" for clarity. Pro Tools, Logic, and most other DAWs have similar Inserts areas for effects, so this should seem pretty comfortable.

The Inserts bin acts as a list of loaded effects. Unlike Pro Tools or Logic, it doesn't have discrete slots for each effect. This is actually an advantage, because you can easily change the order of effects by just dragging them up or down in the list. If you drag an effect, you can position it between two existing effects. This saves time since you don't need to shuffle effects around to open up a slot.

Figure 10-4

There are several controls along the top of each Inserts bin that allow you to add effects, manage FX chains, and turn off all effects in the bin:

FX Chains. The small down arrow to the right of the word "Inserts" opens a menu of preset effects chains. Choose one of these presets to load an entire set of effects into the effects list. There are presets to cover most common mixing setups. In addition you can save your own presets from this menu.

Figure 10-5

Once you have a chain of effects set up the way you like, you can save the entire chain as a preset. Drag from the word "Inserts" on the Effects bin to any folder in the Browser to save the chain. From there, you can rename it and use it again on other channels—even in other Songs. You can drag effects chains from channel to channel to duplicate a setup.

Figure 10-6

Add Effect. This is an alternative to dragging effects over from the Browser. Click on the Plus icon at the top of the Effects bin and select an effect or plug-in from the list. I find that this can be a very quick way to add built-in effects like the Pro EQ, Compressor, or Limiter.

Activate All (Master Power). The Inserts bin header includes a blue power button that works as a master for the power buttons. Click on it to turn the Inserts setup for that channel on and off.

Figure 10-7

Managing Effects

Each effect you drag to a track is represented by a slim FX header in the Inserts bin. As I just mentioned, you can drag a header up to change the effects order. As it does in most DAWs, the audio flows from the top effect down.

Figure 10-8

Opening an Effect Window. Double-click on an effect in the Inserts list to open its full window for greater control. You can also do this by right-clicking on the effect and selecting Edit. The keyboard shortcut F11 also opens the Effect window for whatever channel is currently selected in the Console.

The Effect window for the channel has tabs along the top. If you have multiple effects loaded, you can select which effect you want to work with from these tabs. To cycle through the tabs use Cmd + PageDn or Cmd + PageUp / Ctrl + PageDn or Ctrl + PageUp.

If you want to keep an effect's window onscreen, use the "pin" in the upper right corner to "pin" it in place. This lets you work back and forth between multiple effects without having to switch between them.

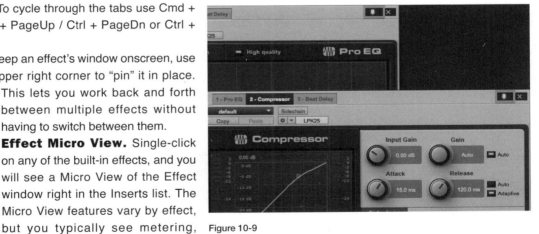

Figure 10-9

Effect Micro View. Single-click on any of the built-in effects, and you will see a Micro View of the Effect window right in the Inserts list. The Micro View features vary by effect, but you typically see metering, frequency plots, and access to key parameters. This feature gives you great control over mixing when you maximize the Console view on a large monitor.

Effect Menu. Click on the small Down Arrow at the left side of the effect name or right-click on the effect name to open the context menu. The context menu gives you several useful actions: Edit, Expand, Rename, Store Preset, and Remove. Edit opens the Effect window.

Expand opens the Micro View. If the Micro View is already open, this option will change to Collapse. Rename allows you to edit the name

Figure 10-10

shown for this instance of the effect. You can use this to clarify the function of the effect, like "LF Cut EQ" rather than just "Pro EQ."

Use Store Preset to save the current setup as a Studio One preset. Third-party plug-ins each has its own preset management that is independent of this function. If you save a preset using this option, it will be available in the Studio One Browser, but not available to other hosts.

Activate (Effect Power). Each effect header has a blue power on/off button. This enables and disables the effect. It is the same as the power button on the Main window for the effect. It is not a bypass button and cannot be automated.

Figure 10-11

Restoring Effects

After you remove an effect, it is saved in the Trash bin (Edit > History > Trash Bin tab). If you want it put it back, open the Trash bin, right-click on the effect, and select Restore. It will return to where you deleted it with exactly the same setting as before. The Trash bin is also available in the Console. Click on Trash over on the left to open the Trash bin panel.

Event Effects

Event effects were introduced with Studio One 2. You can apply effects to individual events. This makes it easy to apply effects to part of a track without needing to add extra tracks or automation. You can also render event effects so they don't use any CPU power. The best part is that you can easily undo the rendering if you want to make changes.

When you enable event effects, you open a full Effects bin for the event, so you can actually put an entire effects chain on an event. If you copy an event that includes event effects, any underlying event effects are all copied along. Since copies are completely new events, you can make separate changes to each.

Figure 10-12

Figure 10-13

Enable Event Effects. Event effects are set up in the Inspector. Select an event and click on the Enable button in the Event FX section.

This opens up an Effects bin. Drag in any effect from the Browser or click on the Add Insert button. Back on the event, a small FX icon shows in the lower right on any event that has event effects enabled.

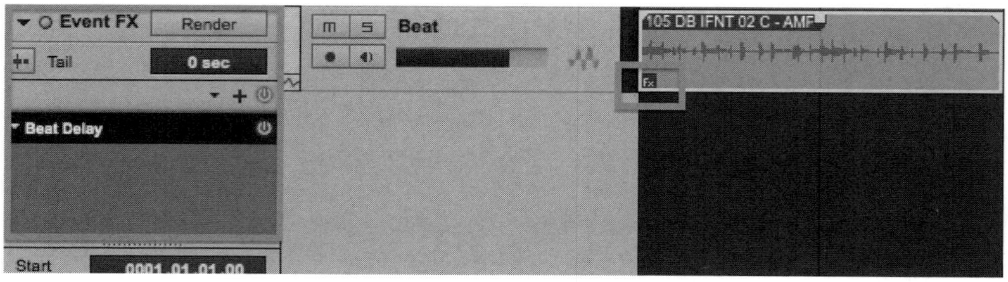

![Event FX render interface screenshot]

Figure 10-14

Render. Once any effect is added, the Enable button changes to say Render. This essentially bounces down the event with its event effects. In a way, it works like the Freeze function. When the effect is rendered, it is taken offline.

Tail / Tail Length. When you try rendering event effects, you will notice that the result is exactly the same length as the original event. This often means that effects like echoes and reverbs get chopped off early. For this reason, you can add some extra time to the event to allow for the effects tail.

Click on the Tail button to enable the event effects tail, and then enter the number of seconds you want to allow for the tail length. If you want to use 200 ms then enter ".2" because the units are in seconds for this property. Note: When you render with a tail, the event will be lengthened accordingly. The tail is essential for allowing you to hear echoes ring out or hear the full reverb tail.

Restore. The Render button becomes a Restore button following rendering. Click on it to bring the effect back online so you can make edits.

Figure 10-15

Figure 10-16

Routing to External FX with Pipeline

Pipeline is one of the built-in effects that allows you to route your audio out to real hardware effects and then back into Studio One on a track or on a bus just as if it were a plug-in. Note: Mixing down and exporting with Pipeline is done in real time because, of course, external hardware only operates in real time.

You can use Pipeline in stereo with any audio interface that has a pair of extra inputs and outputs, or in mono with any device that has one extra input and output.

Configuring Pipeline is easy if you stay organized, keep the software labeling clear, and label your hook-up cables. You can use Pipeline for stereo tracks with left and right or mono tracks.

1. **Name the I/O.** Start by labeling the I/O in Song Setup.

   Clear, straightforward naming really helps. Input and Output naming is done in Options on the Audio I/O tab.

2. **Insert Pipeline.** In the Track Inspector or the console channel, add Pipeline to the Inserts list. When Pipeline opens, assign the Send to the output that you labeled Pipeline Out. Assign Return to the input you labeled Pipeline In.

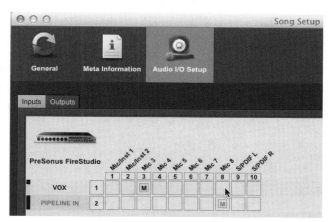

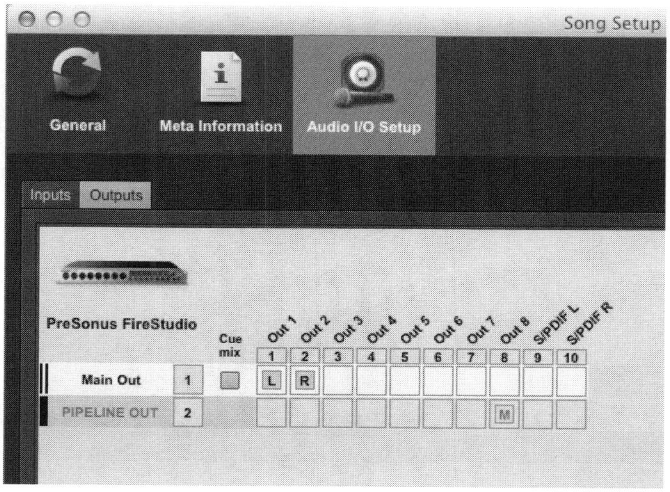

Figure 10-17

Figure 10-18

Figure 10-19

3. **Ping Test.** If your audio interface has a mixer application for input monitoring, make sure that the channel for Pipeline In has been muted or the fader has been turned all the way down. Now, connect a loopback cable between the Pipeline In and Out channels on the interface. For stereo setups, connect separate loopback cables for the left and right channels. Doing a loopback test will verify your routing before you connect the actual effect.

   If the input has a gain control, turn it up somewhat so that when you ping it in the next step you have a chance to see the signal come back through to the input.

   With the loopback cable in place, click on Ping in the Pipeline window. When you do, you should see the metering for the return signal. Click on Re-Ping and adjust the input if necessary. You should also see the Send and Return ping waveforms. Note the color coding. Red is for Send and blue is for Return.

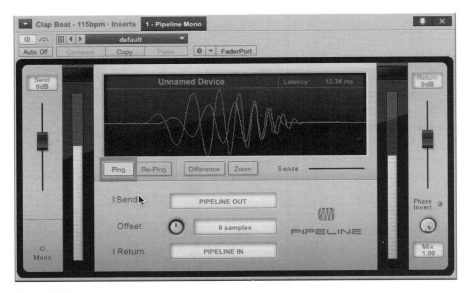

Figure 10-20

4. **Latency Compensation (Offset)**. Next adjust the Offset parameter. You need to optimize this setting to a certain number of samples, depending on your computer and its audio interface settings. The idea is to keep adjusting until the Send (red) and Return (blue) waveforms are in sync. Do this by adjusting the offset parameter in the middle. I usually just double-click on the value and type in guesses and watch the result. On my system this usually comes out to be 20 to 30 samples. For this example, 23 samples was optimum.

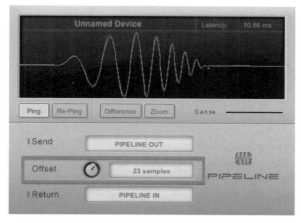

Figure 10-21

5. **Connect the Hardware Effect.** Next connect your actual effect unit. The routing should go out from your interface to the input of the unit, then back from the unit to the input of the interface. You will need left and right paths for stereo units. With this setup you can actually engage Pipeline as an insert effect. Of course you can only have one instance of any specific external hardware unit, but you can bounce down if you want to use it multiple times.

When you're using a physical loop like this, you need to be very aware of the gain stage as it's coming back around into the unit. If red overload lights come on in Pipeline, then you might need to adjust the input gain on your interface or the gain on the hardware.

Chapter 11
ESSENTIAL BUILT-IN EFFECTS

Studio One includes 32 pro-quality, built-in effects. These effects cover a broad range of standard processors, metering, and creative tools. With this comprehensive plug-in support, Studio One can adapt to almost any mixing situation. I don't have the room in this book to get into the details of each effect, but let's take a look at the essential ones.

Channel Strip

Channel Strip is a very useful, nicely designed plug-in. It includes a lowpass filter, a compressor, an expander (which works like a gate), and a concise EQ section. These are the essentials tools for mixing, making this a great general-purpose tool. Channel Strip has a solid selection of presets.

Here is a rundown on the controls:

Low-Cut. Turn on the low-cut (highpass) filter with the LC property, then dial in the frequency. The steep cut is shown graphically. This is perfect for controlling low-end rumble on any kind of track.

Compress. The Compress knob lowers the threshold and increases the ratio as you turn it up. It is very straightforward and effective. Attack and release are determined automatically and are not adjustable. The red LED light comes on when gain reduction is happening.

Note: The Fast, Medium, and Slow controls are not related to attack or release but actually control the speed of RMS averaging for the threshold detection. For most material, you can leave this set to Medium. When compressing low bass signals, the Slow setting might reduce distortion due to the long period of the sound wave. This is a good basic compressor, but if you want more control use the Compressor instead.

Expand. Expand controls a one-knob gate that functions as a downward expander. Use this to cut or reduce hiss and low-level noise.

EQ. The equalizer section of Channel Strip works like a light version of the Pro EQ. Drag left or right to set the frequency and up or down to set the boost or cut. There are also dedicated knobs for each band that are color coded to the nodes on the graph. The high band and low

Figure 11-1

band are shelf filters and the midband is a peaking filter. The Q value is not adjustable. For more precise EQ control, use the Pro EQ effect instead.

Gain and Auto. As you're adding boost and cuts, you can quickly overload the gain. You can adjust the gain manually here, or you can click on Auto here, and Studio One will take care of it for you automatically.

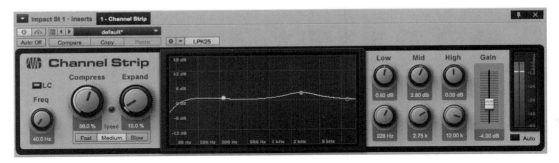

Figure 11-2

Dual Pan

For me, the Dual Pan is an essential tool for mixing. By default, Pro Tools has two pan knobs on stereo channels—one for each side. In Studio One, you can get this same functionality with the Dual Pan effect.

In Studio One, the pan control acts as a balance control for stereo tracks. That means if you pan all the way right, the left channel actually drops out. This is good for level balancing, but for stereo image placement the Dual Pan is more helpful.

Figure 11-3

Use the Input Balance control to balance the levels between the left and right signals. You can position the left and right channels freely with the Left and Right pan knobs. There are also Pan Law options here (if you want even more control over the way the panning scales from left to right) and a Stereo Link.

> **Tip:** The Dual Pan works great if you open the Micro View. This will show you the L and R pan controls right on the channel.

Figure 11-4

Compressor

Compressor is a flexible compressor that can be configured for most compression tasks. It provides clean compression and has clearly labeled controls and excellent visual feedback of the settings and real-time response. Compressor gives you much more control over compression compared with Channel Strip.

Figure 11-5

Ratio. Set the ratio anywhere from 1:1 to 20:1 with the ratio knob or double-click on the value and type in the first part of the ratio. For example, type in "4" for 4:1 or "20" for 20:1. Alternatively, set the ratio by dragging the node on the graph up or down. Ratio values can be set in 0.1 increments, so you have a lot of control. This is especially useful for setting mild compression ratios like 1.5:1.

Threshold. With Threshold fully clockwise, Compressor will not compress at all. Rotate this control counterclockwise until you get the amount of gain reduction you want.

Knee. Compressor has a knee setting that controls the onset of compression around the threshold. It is another control over the ratio that allows the onset of compression to be less abrupt. For standard vocal and instrument compression, a setting of 10 dB works great. For very soft compression you can increase that, or lower it for more dramatic and audible compression.

As you adjust this knob, you will see the effect on the graph. You can adjust the knee by rolling the mouse wheel while pointing at the threshold node on the Compressor graph.

Metering. Compressor has excellent metering including separate input, output, and gain reduction meters. The input meter is vertical and located to the left of the graph display, while the output meter is to the right. The input and output meters indicate peak levels in blue and the RMS level as a white bar. As the signal approaches full scale, the meter indicates red, with a bright red when the Compressor is overloaded.

The gain reduction meter is horizontal and located above the graph. It displays gain reduction with the meter bar moving from right to left.

Look Ahead. Look Ahead is one of several on/off controls that resemble blue LED indicators. When Look Ahead is active, Studio One responds to the threshold 2 ms early. This would be impossible with analog hardware. This is really a fantastic feature to better control transient peaks.

Stereo Link. With Stereo Link turned off, the Compressor operates as a dual mono compressor when applied to stereo signals. With Stereo Link enabled, Studio One will use a mono sum of the left and right channels to trigger the threshold so gain reduction is applied to both channels in exactly the same way.

Input Gain. Adjust the input gain from −12 dB to +20 dB. Use the input meter to calibrate this so you have adequate signal to drive the effect.

Gain. The Gain control is what you probably know as makeup gain. Adjust the output signal to compensate for gain reduction. Gain provides up to an incredible 48 dB of boost, so be careful!

Auto. With Auto engaged the Compressor will automatically compensate for gain reduction and set the makeup gain automatically. Notice that the Gain control is grayed out when Auto is turned on. While this seems like a good idea, you are usually better off to leave Auto turned off and adjust the Gain knob to compensate for gain reduction.

Attack. Attack sets how quickly gain reduction happens after the threshold is reached. With a minimum setting of .10 ms, this is an extremely fast compressor. Combine that with the optional 2 ms Look Ahead, and you can start compression before the signal even happens.

These ultralow settings can be useful for managing transient peaks. In practice, settings between 4 and 10 ms are most common. The attack can be lengthened all the way up to 400 ms.

Release. Release sets the time it takes for gain reduction to go back to 1:1 when the signal goes back below the threshold. It is adjustable between 1 ms and 2,000 ms (2.0 seconds), which is an incredible range. For typical compression tasks, I set this somewhere around 40 to 50 milliseconds.

Auto. The Auto setting automatically adjusts the attack and release times to suit the incoming signal. Use this if you don't know how or don't want to think about setting those controls.

Adaptive. When Adaptive is engaged, the compressor will track the program material and vary the release time to prevent audible pumping. When compressing a full mix, I often leave this control turned on. If you are trying to get a pumping effect, then this should be turned off.

Sidechain. If you activate the Filter control in the Sidechain section, you can apply LC and HC filters to the signal before it goes to the threshold detection circuit. Use this to filter out lows so you can prevent bass frequencies from causing highs to duck. Or tune the filter controls to focus on sibilance and use the compressor as a de-esser. You can hear what you are sending to the Sidechain with the Listen button.

You can select between internal and external sidechain sources. We will talk about external sidechain routing separately. If an external signal is being routed to the compressor, you can use that signal.

One additional feature is Swap. This lets you change the order of the lowpass and highpass filters. It makes for a pretty subtle difference, but sometimes this tweak can help.

Pro EQ

Pro EQ is the full-featured equalizer that's built in with Studio One. It has five parametric equalizer bands along with high-cut and low-cut filters. It features a large frequency-response plot at the center. With no EQ bands engaged, this plot will show a flat horizontal line, indicating that there is no effect on the sound. Each band can be engaged or disengaged using the blue LED-style buttons. As you engage bands you immediately see the result on the plot.

In addition to using the knobs for each band, you can set the filter graphically by grabbing a node on the frequency plot. Drag left or right to set the frequency. Drag up or down to set the boost or cut the gain.

Hold down Shift while dragging to get finer resolution control. Clicking on a node will toggle the band on and off. Use the mouse wheel to adjust the Q.

Here are some details on each of the controls:

Figure 11-6

Current Plot. You can choose between two modes for the plot display: Current and All. With the control set to Current, you see a color coded plot superimposed over the full response plot. This indicates the contribution that band has on the overall plot.

All Plot. With All selected, you see separate color coded plots for each active band. It is an interesting view, but usually Current makes for a cleaner display.

Spectrum Meter Display. You turn on or off a real-time Spectrum display. As it plays back, you'll see the spectrum superimposed. This is helpful because you can see hot spots in the spectrum and the influence of boosts and cuts.

High Quality. The High Quality switch enables 2× oversampling for smooth, precise EQ calculations. You might not hear a lot of difference with this on or off, but I always leave it on. If you need to conserve computing power, you could turn it off.

LC Filter. LC stands for "low-cut." This is a different and probably clearer term for a highpass filter. You can adjust the frequency and pick from a wide range of slopes. The slope ranges from a gentle 6 dB/Oct to a very steep 48 dB/Oct. So this can really take on a lot of different characters. Really nice if you want to roll off the lows to eliminate rumble.

HC Filter. On the opposite end of the scale, we have the high-cut filter. This has similar controls to the low-cut filter.

Parametric Bands. Each of the five parametric bands has the same three controls: Q, Gain, and Freq. In addition the LF (low frequency) and HF (high frequency) bands have filter type controls that allow you to choose between peaking and shelf filters. For shelf filters you can set the slope to 6 dB, 12 dB, or 24 dB. Each band is color coded to the graph, so it is easy to see the contribution of the band to the overall plot.

Limiter

The Limiter effect is an all-around useful limiter. I often put this on the Main Out to control overloads during projects. It works great in this position for mixing and on the Project page during mastering. It has some very helpful features that are not obvious.

Figure 11-7

The Limiter effect includes a high-ratio leveling-style compressor stage and a clipping control called Soft Clip that can be used together to bring up the RMS level of your final mix. While Limiter can't slam tracks has hard as dedicated volume-maximizing tools like Ozone, FG-X, or L2, it can provide a pretty good degree of transparent loudness maximizing along with general-purpose peak control.

Here are the details for each of the controls:

Input. Adjust the input to the limiter. There is excellent metering on the right to show your level. When the input hits the ceiling value, Limiter will prevent the peaks from overloading and you will see gain reduction on the lower meter.

Ceiling. This is the most critical control within Limiter. This sets the level that you don't want the signal to surpass. For basic overload protection, set this to 0 dB. This means limiting occurs at full scale. I often set this with a small safety margin of −0.3 dB. This is really standard practice when mixing to CDs.

Thresh. This humble knob might not be what you think. This is my favorite feature of this effect. Thresh sets the threshold for a secondary 1:20 ratio compressor. Limiter is actually two processors in series: a leveling amp and a brickwall limiter. The compressor section is fixed at a 1:20 ratio so it will get your signal under control, and then any peaks that sneak through will get handled by the limiter.

Release. This is the release time for the limiter. It controls how long it takes for limiting to stop after the signal drops back below the ceiling. The most common setting is 180 ms, but you might want to tweak it to the most transparent option for the tempo of the song.

ISL. The ISL (Intersample Limiter) button changes the ceiling detection to take into account intersample peaks. This is useful for preventing CDs created from your master from distorting when played back on lower-cost consumer gear with cheap digital-to-analog convertor components. If you are mixing for 16-bit CD masters, it is a good idea to use this option if you have Limiter as your final mastering effect. I would usually turn this on for mixing or mastering but leave it off for track processing.

Soft Clip. The Soft Clip button rounds off the square shape of peaks that can result from limiting. With this button engaged, limiting is more transparent, which can be a very good thing when working with digital limiters.

K-System Options. The metering is normally set to PkRMS, giving you peak and average levels. You can alternatively set the meters to any of the K-System references: K-12, K-14, or K-20 if you use Bob Katz's K-System for mixing and mastering.

Open AIR Reverb

Open AIR is a reverb effect that provides a wide range of excellent natural-sounding reverb effects. It is based on convolution, a digital signal-processing technique in which a physical room is sampled with a test tone, speakers, and microphones. The resulting sample is called an impulse response. It essentially encodes the characteristics of the room for use on other sounds. However it works mathematically, this type of reverb sounds very realistic and natural.

Open AIR comes with a wide variety of presets for the most common applications. You can also sample your own impulse responses or use third-party impulses. It also has a lot of settings to tweak the sound, giving a great deal of creative potential. Open AIR is the perfect effect to use for a master reverb when mixing songs.

Figure 11-8

This is what all the controls do:

Presets. Presets are selected like any of the other built-in PreSonus effects. The effects tend toward natural reverb sounds, but other special effects and crazy effects are possible by tweaking the parameters.

Mix. The Mix knob on the right is the most important control in Open AIR. Pick a preset and use Mix to set how much of the reverb is combined with the dry signal. The Mix control is just like the ones you would find on most other effects. When using Open AIR as a master effect on an FX Channel, you will want to turn Mix all the way up to 100%. Like any master effect, it is not good practice to have the dry signal find two paths to the master. A master effect should output only the wet signal, and the dry signal should come only from the sending channel.

Figure 11-9

Predelay. Adjust this between zero and 300 ms. Predelay adds an additional delay before the sound of the impulse response starts. Predelay can help on vocals to avoid getting too much muddiness from a buildup of sound from the reverb, and it also gives you a very strong sense of early reflection.

You can also use Predelay as an effect. If you put in a long predelay, like 180 ms, it will give a slapback effect. This is a common production trick that you can use with any reverb with a predelay setting. You would typically back down on the mix until you are hearing the slap from the predelay with a little reverb on the end. It is a cool effect for guitars and vocals.

You can also set negative values. This actually cuts the beginning of the sample off, meaning that if you have early reflections it will reduce the effect of the early reflections as you dial predelay back. This allows you to reduce the apparent size of a space, allowing you to tailor it to the song and tempo.

Log Time / Log Level. Use the Log Time and Log Level buttons to effectively zoom in on the details of the impulse response waveform. These buttons switch the *x*- and *y*-axis of the waveform plot from linear to logarithmic. This is really helpful for adjusting negative predelay values or adjusting the envelope crossover parameter.

Length. Before explaining the length parameter, I want to point out that the impulse waveform is divided into early reflections (ER) and late reflections (LR). The ER/LR crossover knob lets you set a divider between early and late reflections.

The Length control modifies the late reflections of the impulse. Turning it counterclockwise truncates late reflections with a short fade-out. Turning the control up stretches out the late reflections.

If you turn down the Length, you get a big sense of space but the tail fades off quickly. This is because the early reflections are not affected when the late reflections are being truncated. It's kind of a cool way to get a very dense reverb that is not overpowering. Since turning up length stretches the late reflections, you can finely tune the apparent room size, making it appear bigger without affecting room resonance.

The Shorten with Stretch and Stretch with Pitch options in the Envelope section change the way this control behaves, so read those sections below for more details.

Fade In / Fade Out. The envelope section had fade-in and fade-out controls. These work as you might expect, adding fades to the left and right sides of the impulse waveform. Fade-in allows you to reduce the density of the early part of the reverb. Fade-out can help reduce the tail and works well in conjunction with shortening the Length parameter.

Figure 11-10

ER/LR Crossover. ER/LR Crossover sets the divider between the early/late reflections as I mentioned earlier. Use this especially for imported impulses. Usually you can see the first reflection pretty clearly, but you might need to turn on the Log Time / Log Level display options to see the waveform clearly enough.

Shorten with Stretch. Shorten with Stretch changes what happens when you go negative with the length control. Without this set, negative length just truncates the LRs of the impulse. With this engaged, it uses timestretching to shorten the late reflections. It gives you a different character and in general a much denser sound.

And the interesting thing about this is that because it's not cutting off the end and it doesn't do anything to the early-reflection part of the signal, you still retain the basic character of the space.

Stretch with Pitch. Now an additional modifier is Stretch with Pitch. So rather than using timestretching, it actually uses resampling. The impulse response itself will go up in pitch as you compress it, or it will go down in pitch as you stretch it out.

The effect is a change in the apparent size of the room. Stretch with Pitch also will operate on the ER part of the waveform as you make the length adjustments. It's quite different, allowing you to actually tune the room.

Impulse File. If you single-click on the impulse name, you can browse your file system for additional impulses. Alternatively, just drag them in from the Browser. Many Studio One users obtain impulses sampled from the Bricasti M7, a popular but expensive hardware unit. You can also get impulse responses from a variety of sources online.

Next / Prev. Use the Next and Prev buttons to scroll through any additional impulses that might be in the folder.

Reverb. The Reverb control sets the balance between the early reflections and the late reflections. As you adjust it, you can actually see the effect on the impulse waveform. Turn it counterclockwise to emphasize early reflections and deemphasize the late reflections, and turn it clockwise to do the opposite.

Cross-Feed. Open AIR is not a true stereo reverb, meaning that what goes in on the left side stays on the left side, and what goes in on the right side stays on the right side. Crossfeed controls give you a more natural sense of space when you're dealing with stereo signals.

Figure 11-11

Turn up the crossfeed to send a bit of whatever is coming in on the left to the right side and vice versa.

Cross-Delay. You can also add some delay to the cross-feed. Use it to dial in a sense of size. This works similarly to predelay. This delay can be up to 25 ms. This lets you expand the sense of space, especially with something like acoustic guitar or piano. Most factory presets include some of this delay. If you turn both delay and crossfeed off, the reverb sounds less natural.

Asymmetry. This control gives you the ability to kind of simulate the mic placement being off to one side. I rarely use it but might if I were mixing stereo-miked acoustic instruments that I wanted to mix into a simulated but natural space.

Equalizer. Finally, we have the Equalizer section. The Equalizer offers four bands with a shelf at the low end, a shelf on the high end, and two midbands. On whole, I use the shelves more than anything else. These bands modify the impulse and don't change EQ on your signal directly.

Most of the time, I don't want reverb to be too shimmery on the top, so I roll some high frequencies off using the high shelf. If you're processing a full drum mix and don't really want the kick and bass to be muddied with reverb, then you can roll off the lows.

IR Maker. Studio One Pro also comes with IR Maker. IR Maker is a separate effect that allows you to sample your own impulse responses. Load the effect and follow the steps presented to start sampling your own spaces. It takes some work to capture good impulses, but it's a great tool to get some unique spaces to use in your mixes.

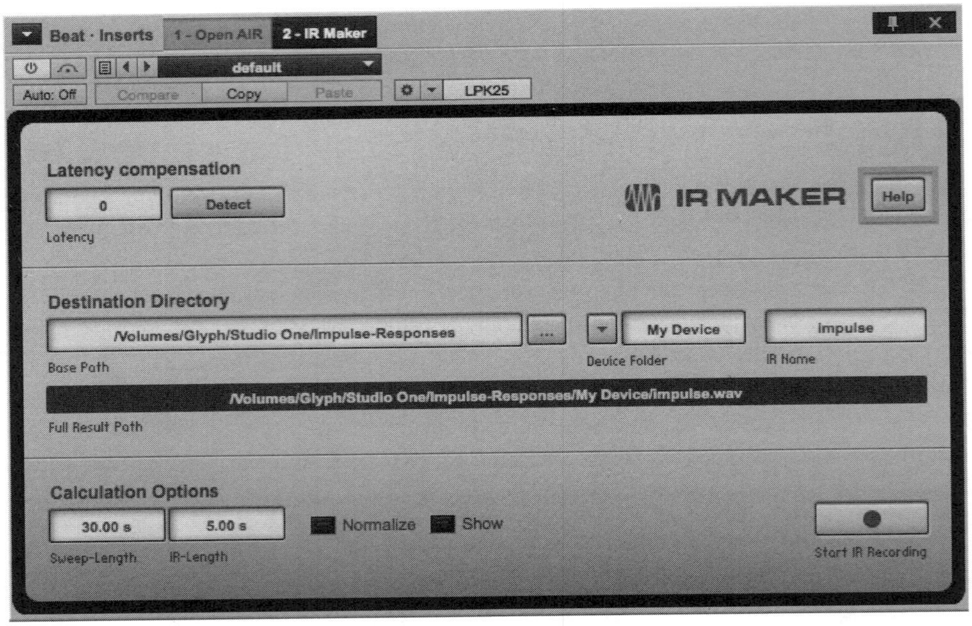
Beat · Inserts
1 - Open AIR
2 - IR Maker
default
Auto: Off
Compare
Copy
Paste
LPK25
Latency compensation
0
Detect
Latency
IR MAKER
Help
Destination Directory
/Volumes/Glyph/Studio One/Impulse-Responses
My Device
Impulse
Base Path
Device Folder
IR Name
/Volumes/Glyph/Studio One/Impulse-Responses/My Device/Impulse.wav
Full Result Path
Calculation Options
30.00 s
5.00 s
Normalize
Show
Sweep-Length
IR-Length
Start IR Recording

Figure 11-12

Chapter **12**
AUTOMATION

S tudio One makes it easy to automate volume, pan, mute, and just about any other parameter from built-in or third-party effects. The Control Link area to the left of the Toolbar gives you direct access to whatever onscreen knob or fader you most recently touched. Just drag the Hand icon to the Arrange view to create an Automation Track for that parameter.

Figure 12-1

Automation can exist as its own track or be added to audio and Instrument Tracks. Automation appears as a color coded envelope that looks like a series of line segments, plotting out the value of the parameter over time.

Automation Basics

In order to see automation for tracks, click on the Show Automation (A) button at the top of the Track header column.

Figure 12-2

Click on the display selector in the Track header to choose from Volume, Pan, or Mute. SONAR users will find this to be very similar to the Edit Filter control in that DAW.

At the bottom of the Automation display list, the Add/Remove option opens the Automation dialog box. From here, you can select automation parameters for the track to add or remove. You can use this to add parameters for effects or virtual instruments.

When you have selected an envelope, you can quickly apply basic automation with the Arrow tool. Just click on the line to add a node, then drag the node to adjust the level. Double-click on a node to delete it. The Info view can be a big help with additional keyboard modifiers. The Paint tool includes a wide range of shapes for editing automation envelopes. I will go into the details later in the chapter.

Figure 12-3

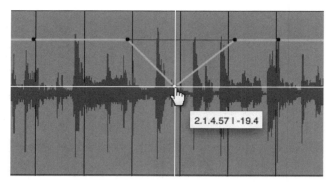

Figure 12-4

Control Link

Control Link makes assigning hardware knobs and faders from your controller very simple. When working with automation, knobs and faders allow you to perform automation, which can lead to more expressive mixes. Before going deeper into the automation modes, let's get up to speed on Control Link.

One of the key features is Focus mapping. This allows you to use the same knob or fader for several different plug-ins or effects. The plug-in with focus onscreen is the one that gets the fader. Global mapping is also available for plug-ins and console controls. With Global mapping, a hardware fader can be assigned only to a single parameter.

Of course, you need a controller with knobs or faders to use this, so make sure you have your hardware installed and configured on the External Devices tab of the Options dialog box (Cmd + Comma / Ctrl + Comma).

Configuring a Control Surface (External Device)

Before you can link hardware knobs to controls in Studio One, make sure your device is set up in Options on the External Devices tab. Either select it from the list or select New Control Surface and enter the name and driver selection.

Figure 12-5

To complete the configuration, open the window for your control surface from the menu on the second Control Link box.

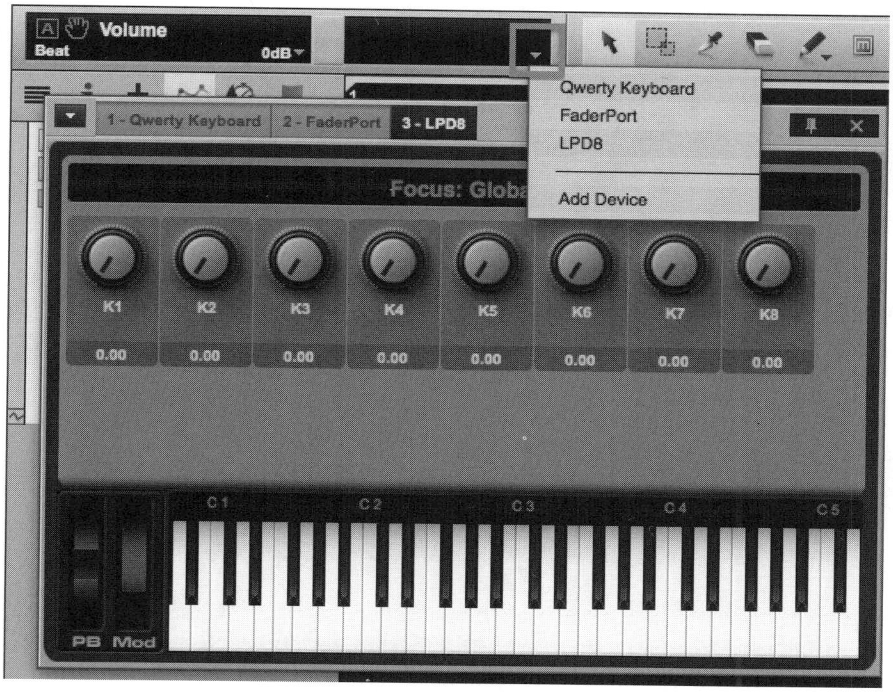

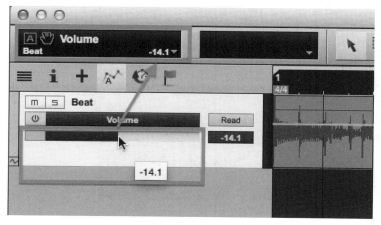

Figure 12-6

Touch each knob and fader on your control surface, until all the controls appear in the window. If you are using a keyboard that includes knobs and faders, you might need to add it as a device twice—once as a keyboard and anther time as a control surface.

Linking Volume, Pan, and Mute to Hardware Knobs

Volume, pan, and mute for tracks and channels can easily be controlled and automated from hardware. Of course you can control and record automation without hardware, but using hardware can offer a better feel when mixing.

To assign a knob or fader, start by moving the onscreen knob a little bit. You will see the parameter listed and the value changing in the left Control Link box.

Figure 12-7

Next, in the right Control Link box, select which hardware controller to use with the small Down Arrow in the lower right corner. A window will open for the controller showing all the available controls as knobs. Next, twist the hardware knob that you want to use for this parameter. The control and its value will be shown in the right Control Link box.

Figure 12-8

Click on the Link icon between the two Control Link boxes to link the onscreen control to the hardware. Now as you turn the knob (or adjust the fader), you will see the change to the parameter onscreen. You can click on the Link icon again to turn this off.

Figure 12-9

When you use Control Link to map channel volume, pan, or mute, it is a global map. The knob or fader will continue to control that parameter and nothing else until you unlink it.

Linking Effects Parameters to Hardware Knobs

For effects parameters, access the Control Link Setup boxes in the Effect window for the plug-in by clicking on the Gear icon. This works the same on virtual instruments as well.

Figure 12-10

The steps are the same as for channel and track controls:
1. Wiggle the onscreen control to map.
2. Wiggle the hardware knob.
3. Click on the link between the Control Link boxes to map the hardware to the software.

Now the hardware knob will control the effect parameter as long as the window is open.

Focus Mapping

The cool thing about Control Link is that you can reuse your hardware knobs throughout Studio One with Focus mapping. Enable Focus mapping at the top of any effect or instrument window by clicking on the controller selection until it turns yellow. Focus mapping is enabled by default, so you usually only need to check that the box is yellow.

Figure 12-11

With Focus mapping, knobs on your controller are available to whatever window you have open onscreen. The benefit is that you can freely assign and reuse knobs on many different effects.

Global Mapping

Global mapping is the alternative to Focus mapping. With Global mapping, when you assign a parameter to a knob, the knob will adjust that parameter regardless of what window you have open. This is great if you want to record automation for several parameters across multiple effects. The downside is that hardware knobs are mapped to software controls on a one-to-one basis. This means you can use a knob for only one thing at a time.

To use Global mapping for effects or virtual instruments, click on the controller selection to turn off the yellow highlighting. If you want to unlink a knob, wiggle it then click on the Unlink button between the Control Link boxes.

Figure 12-12

Note: If you have a plug-in or virtual instrument open with Focus mapping enabled, none of the Global mapping for that hardware will work. Focus mapping takes precedence over anything that you might have globally mapped.

Recording Automation

Let's get into how to record automation in real time. Let me point out that you don't actually need any hardware controllers to record automation. You can record automation by tweaking onscreen parameters with the mouse. Many engineers just feel better if a hardware knob or fader is involved.

There are several modes that you can use for recording automation. You can set the automation mode in several places:

1. On the Track header when Show Automation (A) is enabled.

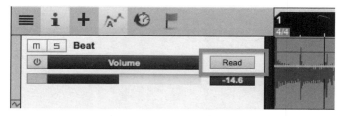

Figure 12-13

2. Using the Track Automation property in the Inspector.

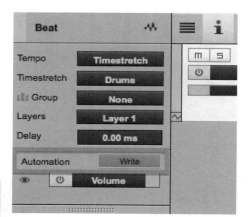

Figure 12-14

Figure 12-15

3. On the channel just below the fader.

Next, let's go over how the different automation modes work:

Auto: Off. This mode disables automation. If you have automation recorded, it will be ignored.

Read. This mode enables the automated playback of any automation recorded on the track. After you record automation, put the automation into this mode to hear the results during playback.

Touch. This is a variation on Write mode (covered soon). It changes the recorded automation if you change a parameter during playback. This is similar to Write mode but is usually used for making minor changes to automation you have already recorded. You don't need to hit Record to record automation in Touch mode.

Latch. This mode is another variation on Write mode. Latch will keep the value at the final setting and continue to write it until you stop playback.

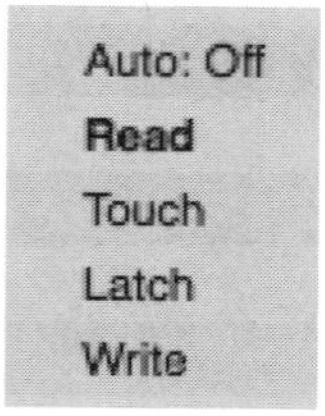

Auto: Off
Read
Touch
Latch
Write

Figure 12-16

I use this mode for performing transitions from one section to the next in which you want to move to a new volume level.

Write Mode. This is the primary mode for recording automation. Select or add the controller you want to automate, enable Write mode, place the cursor where you want automation, and hit Play. There is no need to hit Record. When you finish recording the automation, set the track to Read as you listen back to what you have done.

Editing Automation

You can edit automation envelopes right in the Arrange view. Make sure Show Automation (A) is enabled, and select which envelope to edit using the automation display list on any track.

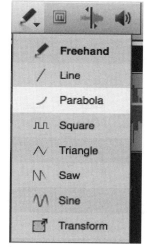

Figure 12-17

Automation editing is done using the mouse tools. Here is the rundown for each tool:

Arrow Tool. Basic editing of envelope nodes is done with the Arrow tool. As I mentioned before, Info view is extremely helpful for understanding all the mouse tool modifiers. Here are the essentials for working with automation nodes:

- Click to add a node.
- Double-click to delete a node.
- Drag a node left or right along the Timeline or up and down to adjust the value. Drag is affected by the current Snap and Quantize settings.
- Click on an existing node to select it. Shift-click to add additional nodes to the selection.
- Right-click to access the context menu. Here, you can edit the node value directly or delete it. Cut and copy are also available. They are useful for moving or copying a selection.
- Press Cmd-click / Ctrl-click to reset a node to the default value.

Range Tool. Use the Range tool to select a range of nodes. Drag the selection to move it or hit Delete to remove all the nodes. The normal cut, copy, and paste commands work here as well.

Eraser Tool. Click on a node with the Eraser tool to delete it. This works but is not all that necessary. Double-clicking on a node with the Arrow tool also deletes it, and so does selecting a node and clicking on Delete.

Paint Tool. The Paint tool has all kinds of cool variations for drawing and editing automation envelopes. Select which type of Paint tool is active by clicking on the Paint Tool icon. The current selected type is shown in the Toolbar. Let's go over the types.

Figure 12-18

As you draw with any of the Paint tools, adding Shift will toggle the snap state. Here are the variations on the Paint tool:

- Freehand is the default paint tool. Click-and-drag with this tool to draw in automation the way you would with a pencil. The Freehand tool respects the current Snap and Quantize settings. As you draw with Snap on, nodes will be placed only on the grid. With Snap off, you can draw more complex curves made from lots of nodes.
- Use the Line tool to draw in line segments. This works great for simple fades or level adjustments. To move a line segment, hold down Opt / Alt and drag.

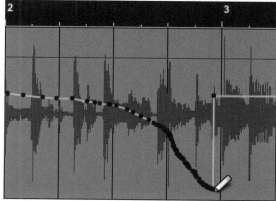

Figure 12-19

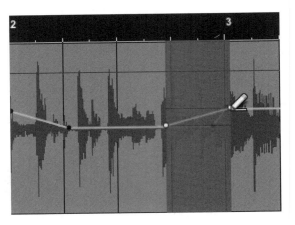

Figure 12-20

- Use the Parabola tool to draw in a parabolic curve, sweeping up or down from the starting node. The curve is actually constructed from discrete nodes and is not affected by the Snap setting.

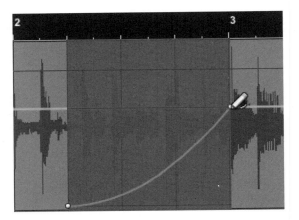

Figure 12-21

- Use the Square, Triangle, Saw, or Sine tools to draw repeating shapes as indicated by the tool name. The Quantize setting determines the width of the cycle. As you paint in these shapes dragging up and down affects the depth of the shape. The starting vertical position has a big effect on how you can drag the shape, so experiment with that. With Snap on, the starting node will be lined up to the grid.

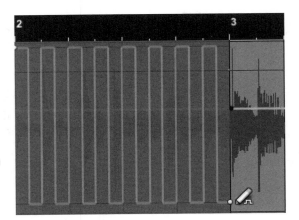

Figure 12-22

- The Transform tool is the coolest way to modify automation envelopes. Drag a Transform box around a group of nodes, and drag it up or down to offset them. Reshape the box to scale the automation, warp it, or distort it. Transform is a great way to offset the level of existing automation shapes.

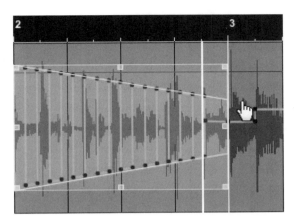

Figure 12-23

Automation Follows Events

In general, Automation is a Track property. As you move Events around, the automation stays in place. However, if you have carefully crafted an automation envelope over an event, you probably want the automation to go with the event if you move it or duplicate it. For that reason, there is an option to allow automation to follow an event if you move it. The setting "Automation follows events" is located on the Options dialog box under Advanced > Automation. I almost always keep this setting enabled.

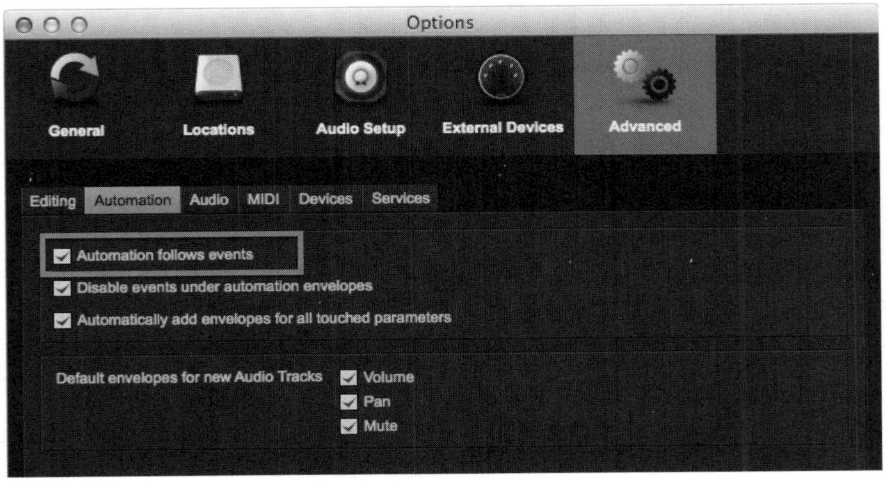

Figure 12-24

Chapter 13

MIXING AND EXPORTING

Track Transform

Often, when you're dealing with high track counts and lots of effects you start to increase the device block size to get clean playback leading to latency and general slowness. With high track and plug-in counts, you might reach the limits of your CPU power.

You can help solve this problem with Track Transform, a feature similar to "track freeze" in other systems. Track Transform allows you to temporarily render effects and virtual instruments to conserve CPU power. "Render" is another way to say "mix down."

Transforming (Freezing) Audio Tracks

To transform an Audio Track, right-click on the Track header and select Transform to Rendered Audio. This is also available from the menu Track > Transform > Transform to Rendered Audio. This is available only if you have effects inserted on the channel.

A dialog box appears with two options: Preserve Realtime State and Tail.

Preserve Realtime State. Preserve Realtime State allows you to undo the Track Transform. Normally, you want this enabled. At any time after you use Track Transform, you can use Transform to Realtime Audio from the right-click menu on the track to return the track to its original state.

Tail. This option lengthens rendered events that have reverb or delay effects, so that the echoes aren't abruptly cut off at the end of the event. Each event will be lengthened and crossfaded, which can make it a little hard to work with. Because of this, it is wise to bounce the track to a single event before transforming it.

Figure 13-1

Figure 13-2

Transforming Instrument Tracks

This feature works the same way as it does for Audio Tracks, except there are a few more options and transforming is done by selecting Transform to Audio Track. Since the result is audio, this will bounce to a new Audio Track and remove the Instrument Track.

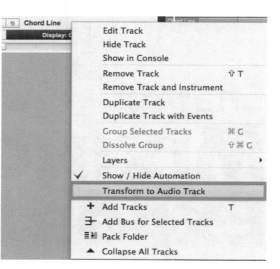

Figure 13-3

Render Inserts. With Instrument Tracks you have an option to render the insert effects along with the instrument. When mixing, I often want to render the instrument but leave the effects in real time for additional tweaking. The effects often use less CPU power than the instrument itself. Click on Render Inserts if you want the bounced files to include the effects.

Preserve Instrument Track State. You can get the original instrument back with Transform to Instrument Track if you click on Preserve Instrument Track State. Normally, you will select this option.

Figure 13-4

Remove Instrument. When you transform with this option selected, the instrument is removed from the Song, freeing both CPU and memory loads.

Tail. This parameter works just the way it does for Audio Tracks and is necessary to use if you have insert effects on the track that play out for a while.

Channel. Many virtual instruments have multiple output channels. Choose which channel to use for the transform with this parameter.

Bouncing Events

Bouncing events is the process of converting separate events in one track to a single event. This is an essential editing task and works slightly differently for Audio Events and Instrument Parts.

Bouncing Audio Events

Select a group of Audio Events using the Arrow tool or the Range tool, and then hit Cmd + B / Ctrl + B. A new single event replaces the selection. If you have selected events on several tracks, the events in each track will be bounced separately.

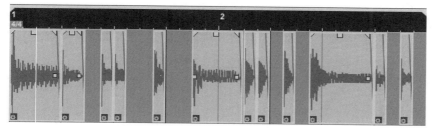

Figure 13-5

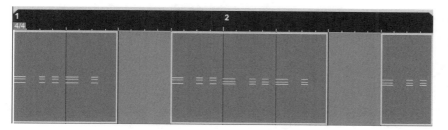

Figure 13-6

Bouncing Instrument Parts

If you select one or more Instrument Parts and hit Cmd + B / Ctrl + B, then the Instrument Part is bounced to a new audio channel and the original track is muted.

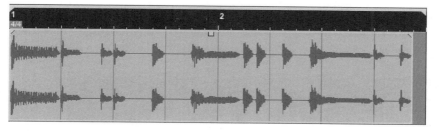

Figure 13-7

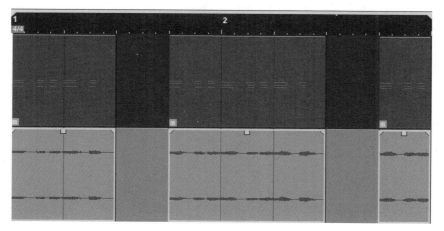

Figure 13-8

Audio Parts / Audio Loops

Turning a track into an Audio Part has an effect similar to bouncing it. The difference is that in an Audio Part, the events still remain and can be moved around, so an Audio Part basically functions as a container for events.

Creating Audio Parts

To create an Audio Part, select the events on the track and press G (Audio > Merge to Audio Part). You can now use the Audio Part as though it were an event.

The Chain Link icon in the lower left corner indicates that it is an Audio Part. You will also notice that it doesn't have fade or volume handles, since there are multiple events within the Audio Part.

To see the component events, double-click on the Audio Part to open the editor.

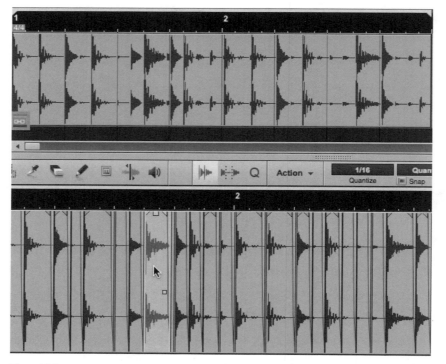

Figure 13-9

Drum Loops as Audio Parts

Using Audio Parts is an excellent way to handle drum loops, and is similar to using REX files. In fact, if you import a REX file, Studio One converts it to an Audio Part. You can load an Audio Part into the SampleOne instrument by selecting Audio > Send to SampleOne. This loads an Instrument Track and SampleOne with the slices mapped across the keyboard and ready to play!

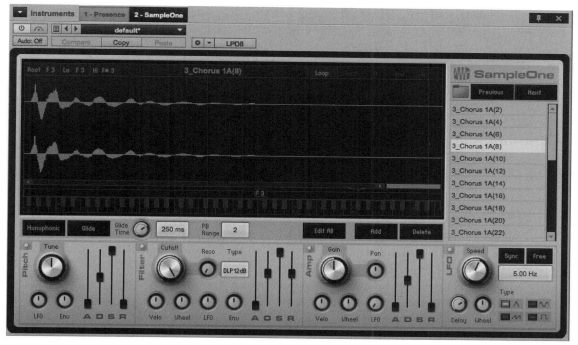

Figure 13-10

A great way to create a new Audio Part from a loop is to use the Audio Bend panel to detect the transients and then select the Slice option and click on Apply. This will slice each drum hit into separate events. Select all the events and hit G to make it into an Audio Part. Double-click on the part to access or move the individual slices in the Editor. The individual hits will now be easy to move around and edit.

Duplicating Audio Parts

Audio Parts are very useful for arranging loops, because you can simply hit the D key to duplicate what would otherwise be several events, but still edit the individual slices if you need to.

Pressing Shift + D will create a shared duplicate of an Audio Part. This type of duplication just creates a reference to the original Audio Part, so if you make changes to one, they will all change. This can be very cool for a drumbeat that runs throughout the song: make a change to the first loop, and the entire Song is updated with the new version.

Creating Audio Loops

An Audio Loop is a PreSonus-designed file type that has the .audioloop extension. If you search the Browser on the Sounds tab for "audioloop," you will find that much of the included content in Studio One is in the Audio Loop format.

You can think of Audio Loops as REX files without the restrictions. To create an Audio Loop file, just drag any Audio Part to the Browser and it will be exported as an .audioloop file by default. When you drag it back into a Song, it becomes an Audio Part, with all the slices ready to edit in the Editor.

Figure 13-11

Audio Part Play Modes

We've already established that Audio Parts are made up of numerous event slices. Since those slices can overlap, there are several modes for how to handle overlaps and timestretching. To see the available modes, select an Audio Part and check out the event properties in the Inspector view.

Here is how each mode works:

Stretch Events. This option determines if the slices will stretch to match tempo based on the track Timestretch setting. With this turned on, Audio Parts behave much like a normal Audio Event. The following modes are more useful when you turn Stretch Events off!

Figure 13-12

Normal Mode. In Normal mode, if slices overlap, only the slices on the top will play.

Overlaps Mode. Overlaps mode allows each slice to play out, even if it overlaps with the next event. If the audio sounds too choppy, Overlaps mode might work better. It's easy to test the different modes to see what works best.

Slices Mode. If you speed the tempo up with Stretch Events turned off, the slices can overlap. When you use Slices mode, quick fades are automatically added to reduce the chance of popping and clicking.

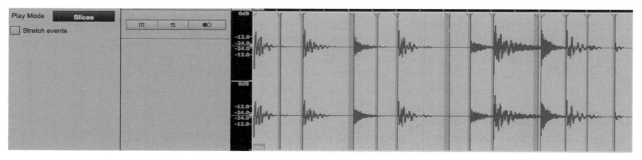

Figure 13-13

If you slow the tempo down, the slices get spaced apart more. Since the audio is not stretched, you don't get the degradation of quality you might with other methods. The Slices mode works really well for Audio Loops—especially ones that are percussion oriented—because as you stretch or compress, it still sounds nice and clean.

Exporting Stems

Export stems is one of the most important things to learn if you are using Studio One at a professional level. It allows you to export tracks and submixes for use in other DAWs.

You can export stems with drag-and-drop to the Browser or the Export Stems dialog box. The Export Stems dialog box (Song > Export Stems) allows you to export from either tracks or channels, for a total of three different export methods—each one with a slightly different signal path.

Drag and Drop

The easiest way to export audio from Studio One is by dragging an Audio Event to the Browser. Doing this creates a WAV file, bypassing the channel settings, insert plug-ins, and Main Out. Only the event itself is exported. Note that the Track Stereo/Mono property is exported with this method, so make sure you have that set correctly.

To prepare for a drag-and-drop export, bounce all the events on a track to one continuous event by hitting Cmd + B / Ctrl + B. You probably want the events to start from the time zero if you plan to import into another system so that all of the tracks will sync correctly. To do this, select the events in the track with the Range tool and drag the selection all the way to zero. Now when you bounce the event, it will start at zero—even if nothing is playing at that point. This isn't restricted to a single track, either. Select events across as many tracks as you like, and drag them over at once.

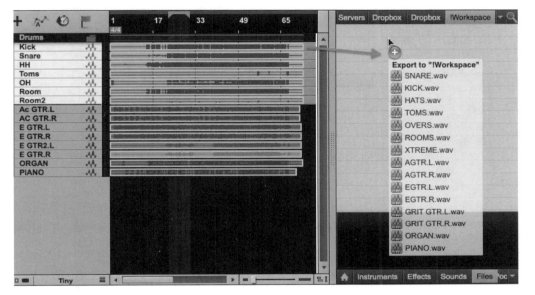

Figure 13-14

Export Stems Dialog Box

You can bring up the Export Stems dialog box by hitting Shift + Cmd + E / Shift + Ctrl + E (Song > Export Stems). When you export using the Export Stems dialog box, the files are placed in the Stems folder for the Song by default.

Export Tracks. The left side Tracks tab lists every track in Arrange view including hidden tracks and tracks inside Folder Tracks. When you select a track from the list, it is soloed and mixed down with insert effects, send effects, and the master bus. If you select multiple tracks, it will render them one at a time, in succession, through the entire Console and all the effects.

Figure 13-15

Figure 13-16

Export Channels. If you use the Channels tab, you will export through the output of the selected channel. There are several options for what to include: the Main Out, Bus Channels, virtual instruments, and effects channels. You must use the Channels tab to export stems from the bus, FX, and Instrument Channels since they are not represented in Studio One as tracks.

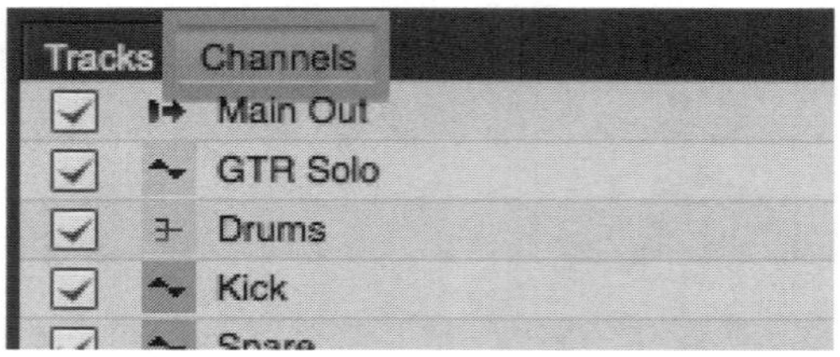

Figure 13-17

Export File Location and Name. By default, stems will export to a Stems folder that is stored with the Song files. If you want, you can give each stem a name. This will be the prefix in the filename, followed by the track or channel name.

You can export stems to SoundCloud if you select that option next to Publishing. It is much more likely you would want to do this from the Export Mixdown dialog box, which I will cover in more detail in a later section.

Figure 13-18

Format. Select the output file format including file type, resolution, and sample rate. The format options vary depending on file type.

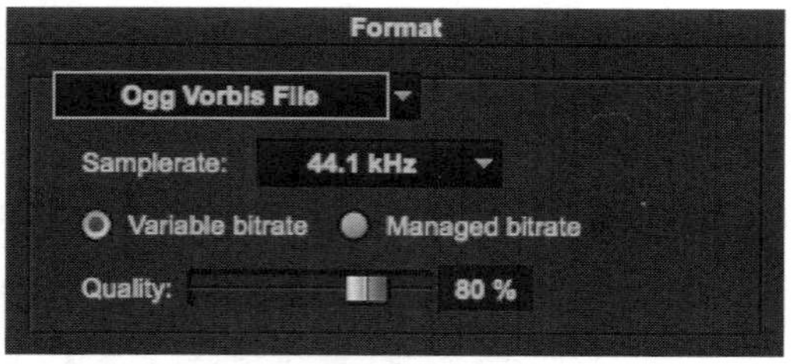

Figure 13-19

File Format	Properties
WAV	Resolution, Sample rate
AIFF	Resolution, Sample rate
FLAC	Resolution, Sample rate, Compression level
Ogg Vorbis	Sample rate, Variable or Managed bit rate, Quality
MP3	Bit rate, Sample rate

Export Range. There are four options for what part of the Timeline to include in the export. The first two options, Between Loop and Between Song Start/End Marker, are the most common.

- Between Loop will export the whole range between the loop in and out points. To set the loop over the entire song, use Cmd + A / Ctrl + A to select all events, then hit P to set the loop over the selection.
- Between Song Start/End Marker will export the full song as defined by the start and end markers placed correctly.
- Between Each Marker is useful if you have multiple songs in the same Song file. Mark the beginning of each song, and this will break the export into separate sets of files for each song region.
- Between Selected Markers works the same way as Between Each Marker but allows you to pick a single marker to marker range for the export.

Figure 13-20

Tip: Set the End Marker in the Marker Track by dragging the end flag to line up with the end of the song. It helps to turn on Cursor Follows Edit Position. With this on, the cursor will follow the flag and you can use it to accurately align to the song end.

Duration. This is the calculated duration and is view only. It can help you make sure the output is as long as you expect it to be.

Options

There are several additional options available when exporting stems. These are grouped in the Options section of the Export Stems dialog box and give you more control over what happens during the export process:

Preserve Mono Tracks. With this selected, any mono tracks or channels will export to mono files. With this deselected, everything will export as stereo files. Mono files will convert to dual mono stereo files.

Import to Track. With Import to Track selected, all the exported audio files are imported as new tracks right back into the Song.

Figure 13-21

Sometimes this can be a really useful production technique—for example, mixing down through an effect and then bringing it back into the track for additional processing.

Close After Export. This option simply closes the dialog box after the export is finished. Leave this off when you have several exports to do and you don't want to keep reopening the dialog box.

Overlap. Overlap is important only if you select Between Each Marker in the Export Range area. This adds a little extra time before and after each range.

Mixdown

Once you have the song balanced with effects applied and you're happy with the way it sounds on playback, the final mixdown is very easy. The following topics serve as a checklist leading up to the final mix.

Main Out Effects

What you should put on the Main Out (stereo bus) is a topic of much debate. If you are mixing for someone else to master, I would suggest putting as little as possible on the Main Out. If you are going to master in the Studio One Project page, then you probably also want to put very little processing on at this stage. If you are mixing for upload or playback in your car, or for your own entertainment, then you can freely apply mastering effects at this stage.

Figure 13-22

In any Event, it is not a bad idea to put a limiter on the master to protect against any potential peaks.

For basic master bus limiting, I typically set the ceiling on the limiter to 0.3 dB as a safety net. Personally, this is really all I would normally add to the master. I adjust the mix levels so that this limiter never or barely ever causes the limiter to indicate gain reduction.

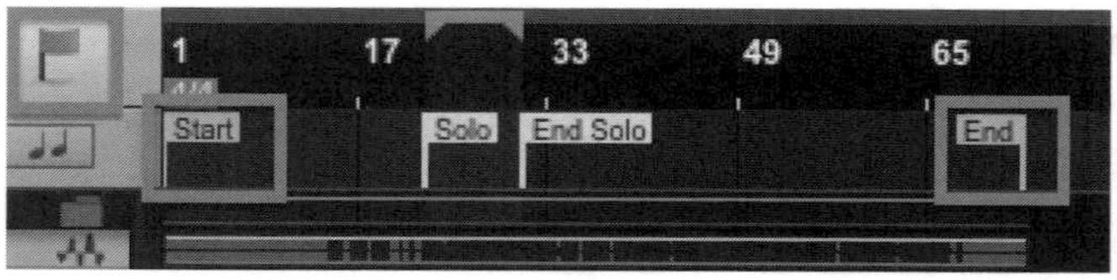

Setting Song Length

It is a good idea to check the song length before mixdown. If it's set correctly, you can use it as the export range in the Export Mixdown dialog box. It will also make the Song transfer to the Project page with the correct length.

To set the song length, open the Marker Track and drag the end flag to match the end of the Song. Zoom in or turn on Cursor Follows Edit Position to make sure you position the end flag correctly.

Figure 13-23

Mixing Down

To actually mix down a Song, select Song > Export Mixdown. This should look really familiar; the properties are exactly the same as the right-hand side of the Export Stems dialog box. When you press OK, the song will be mixed down and placed in the Mixdown folder of the Song.

Typically, the mixdown will be done much faster than in real-time. You will enjoy this if you were working with other DAWs that required you to wait for the entire tune to play (Pro Tools, for example!). You can do mixdown in real time if you have external processing active through Pipeline or just have extra time on your hands by activating Realtime Processing in the Options section. For the details of the other options, see the descriptions in the Export Stems section just before. The options work exactly the same.

Figure 13-24

PART IV: STUDIO ONE PROFESSIONAL MASTERING AND RELEASING

Chapter 14

THE PROJECT PAGE

The Project page is the place to create albums of multiple songs and set the Track order, make Track-to-Track spacing, balance levels, apply fades, and master effects. Here, you can create Red Book CD masters as well as release to a variety of digital formats including SoundCloud, disc images, and DDP.

Overview

You can import audio files into the Project page by drag-and-drop. This means you can use Studio One for mastering even if the songs were not recorded and mixed in Studio One.

However, one of the coolest aspects of the Project page is the integration with Studio One Songs. A mix from the Song page becomes a Track in the Project page. There is a round-trip connection between Songs and Tracks that allows you to easily rerender a mix from the Project if anything has changed since the last session. This makes the Project page into a work-in-process hub for recording albums or songwriting.

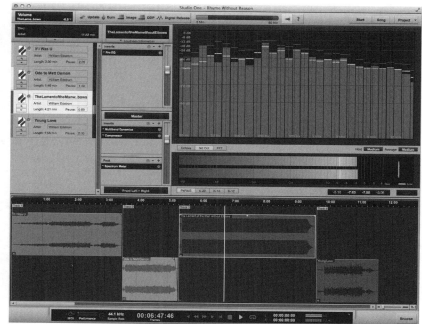

Figure 14-1

You can expand and collapse most areas of the Project page by dragging the borders between sections. You can also double-click on the borders in the Inserts area to expand or collapse the views. Here is a summary of each of the main areas of the Project page:

Track Column. Tracks in a Project are listed in the Track Column to the left. You can change the Track order by drag-and-drop. Import Song files or audio files from the Studio One Browser or your file system. You can control Track-to-Track spacing with the Pause property. Pause sets the amount of silence between the Track and the previous Track for CD mastering.

Timeline. Tracks appear automatically staggered on the Timeline. This makes editing a crossfaded Track easier. Much of the editing here works the way it does in the Studio One in the Song page, so you should feel comfortable quickly. There is no mouse tool selection, but what you have is essentially the Arrow tool. Drag the edges to resize, fade, or apply gain boosts or cuts.

Browser. The Project page Browser has only two main tabs—Effects and Files. Use the Files tab to drag in Studio One Songs or other audio files. Use the Effects tab to drag mastering effects to individual Tracks or the Master Output.

Project Page Fundamentals

The Project page can work as the main center of any Project with multiple Songs. Don't feel you need to wait to get all your mixes done before creating a Project and linking your Songs to it. I usually get the Project started as soon as I start the first song of an album. When I work on tracking or mixing, I start from the Project page as an overview of the album. At any point I can create MP3s or CDs of the work in progress to check by listening to them in my car.

Adding Songs

If you open any Studio One Song folder, you will find the actual .song file. This is the file you want to drag over when adding a Song to the Project.

Figure 14-2

After you drag it to the Project, you will be prompted to update the mastering files. Click on OK and Studio One will load that Song, render a mix, and add it as a Track to the Project.

If the Track appears in the Project with a lot of extra time at the end, it means you didn't have the Song End Marker set correctly. You can easily correct it by just grabbing the right edge in the Timeline and trimming it back. However, it's probably better to go to back into the Song and correctly place the End Marker. You can easily go back into the mix of any Song by just clicking on the Wrench icon. This allows you to open that Song to tweak the mix without ever even closing the Project. Just click on the Project button in the upper right to return to the Project page.

Syncing Songs and Projects

If a Track appears in the Project with a red indicator, that means changes have been made to the mix since the mastering file was last updated—basically, the Song and Project are out of sync. To resync, click on the red light. Studio One will quickly rerun the mix and update the mastering file for that Track.

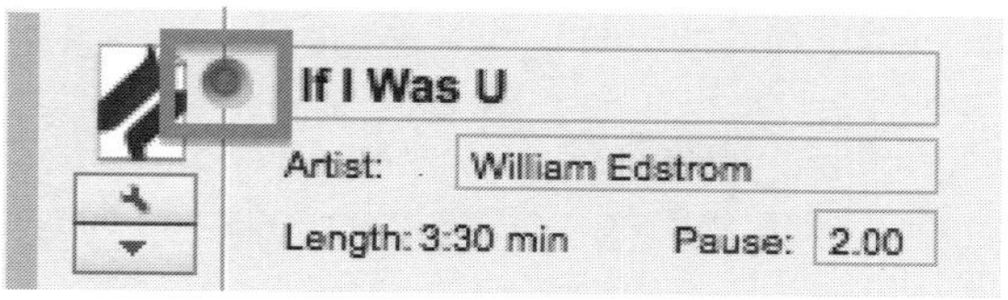

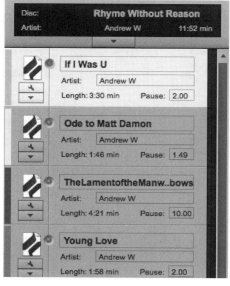

Figure 14-3

Project Page Toolbar

The Project page Toolbar has fewer controls than the Song page. Let's take a look at what's here:

Figure 14-4

Control Link. The first two boxes on the left are for Control Link. Just as in the Song page, you can map hardware knobs and faders to onscreen controls in the Project page. Note: the Project page doesn't support automation. Hardware knobs and faders are useful for setting levels and plug-in parameters. All of this essentially works the same as in the Song page.

Update. The Update button will allow you to quickly update the mastering files for any of the Tracks that are out of sync between the Song and the Project. Those are the ones indicated by a red light. Deselect any file you don't want to update. After you click on OK, it loads each Song, rerenders the mix, and updates the mastering files. When everything is done it returns to the Project page and everything is in sync.

Burn. Burn allows you to burn Red Book–spec CDs. I will go into more detail on this a bit later.

Image. Image is another way to export a master from the Project page. Some mastering facilities will use an image file for CD manufacturing. You can also use these files with other ISO-CD CD-burning applications. Since you get a full-length audio file, it is also a great way to assemble a podcast from segments.

DDP. Disc Description Protocol is the current standard for CD manufacturing. This feature creates a folder of files that includes everything needed to manufacture discs.

Digital Release. A digital release is typically used to create a set of MP3 files to be hosted online through any of the popular services. In addition, you have the option to upload directly to SoundCloud.

Project Length Meter. The meter area here shows you how much space your album would use up on a typical Red Book audio CD. The maximum length allowed is 79.8 minutes. If a Project gets too long, the meter goes red to warn you that you've got too much content for an audio CD.

Working with Tracks

Keep in mind that a "Track" on the Projects page is actually an entire song. The list of Tracks is called the Track Column in Studio One. The Track Column is automatically synced with the Timeline, and many things can be done in either place. The layout is very straightforward,

Figure 14-5

and it makes Studio One the easiest mastering and releasing tool available. So let's go over how to work with the Track Column and Tracks:

Album Header. At the top of the Track Column you will find disc and Artist properties. These are properties that apply to the entire album, but most of the properties can be set Track-by-Track as well.

Click on the Down Arrow to expand this section and show all the metadata. Metadata values set at the Track level take precedence. The calculated length is shown but not editable.

Track Order. You can rearrange Tracks by grabbing them and moving up or down in the list. This makes it very easy to sequence an album. Notice that the Timeline reflects the change instantly as you move Tracks.

Track Properties

The header for each Track contains all the properties needed to define a song and its position on an album. Here are the details:

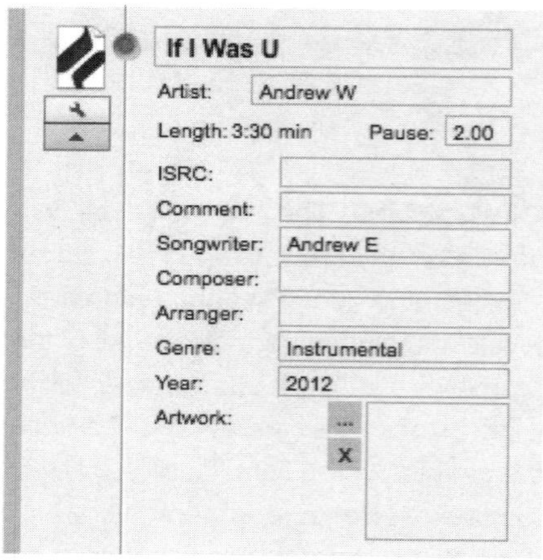

Track Name / Artist / Length. The Track name and artist are imported from the Studio One Song, but you can also edit those here. The Length shows the Track length and will change if you trim the Track in the Timeline area.

Pause. This value sets the pause before the Track. You will need to leave the first Track in the Project set to zero. Track-to-Track pauses can really change the emotional impact of the album. Typically, you want the pauses to be between one and two seconds. Bear in mind that this was more important when people actually listened to CDs; Track-to-Track pause settings are lost in iTunes.

Figure 14-6

Track Metadata. Click on the Down Arrow at the left of the Track to expand the header and show additional Track data properties, called metadata. Appropriate fields of metadata will be transferred to the released files depending on how you release. For example, these fields will transfer to the ID3 tags for MP3 files or to the upload data to SoundCloud.

If you entered this information in Song Setup on the Song page, it will already be populated when you get to this point. Before releasing you can fill in missing data or make corrections.

Edit a Song and Resync. Click on the Wrench icon to open the Track's Song page. Make any mix corrections in the Song page and save. When you come back to the Project page, the red indicator will signal that the mastering file is not up-to-date. Click on the red light on the Track or hit Update on the Toolbar to resync the Project and Song. This workflow is unique to Studio One, and after you get used to it, it is hard to live without!

Track Right-Click Menu

There are some useful actions available by right-clicking on a Track. Edit Song and Update Mastering File are repeated here, but there are some other important actions we haven't encountered until now:

Show in Finder. This action locates the mastering file on your computer and opens the folder in Finder (Mac) or Explorer (Windows). The mastering file is part of the

Figure 14-7

actual Song folder structure in a subfolder called Master. Mastering files are not stored with the Project; rather, they are stored with the Song.

Remove Track. This takes a Track out of the Project. Undo (Edit > Undo) will bring it back if this happens in error. Another way to remove a Track is to click on it in the Timeline area and hit Delete.

Disable Track. When you disable a Track, it appears with a red warning and disappears from the Timeline. I find this useful when I have a reference tune loaded into the Project. I can take it offline so it doesn't get published without removing it, in case I want to refer to it again.

Detect Loudness. This runs a process on the mastering file for the Track that reports useful statistics about the loudness.

The results appear right of the Track Column in the Loudness Information drop-down menu. It shows the calculated dynamic range (DR) and the loudness in LKFS (Loudness, K-weighted, relative to Full Scale) units. You also see left and right channel peak, RMS, and DC offset values here. Detect Loudness does not take into account any effects applied on the Project page; rather, it strictly looks at the mastering file—essentially the mix from the Song page.

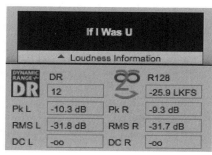

Figure 14-8

> **Tip:** Matching the LKFS between Tracks is a helpful check on your levels to make sure songs are similar in loudness. If you tweak each mix to get the loudness close, mastering gets much simpler!

Project Page Effects Inserts

In the Project page you can apply effects at the Track level or the master level. Master effects can be applied before and after the master fader. Each Track has its own effects inserts. Let's break down how these all work together:

Track Effects Inserts

Each Track has an Inserts bin that works like the Inserts in the Console view. This is called a "Device Rack" in the manual. Other systems call this an "effects bin" or simply "Inserts." When you click on a Track, the Inserts bin displays the inserts for that Track. The parts of the Inserts bin are similar to the Inserts bin in the Console view.

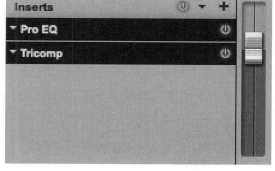

Effects Chains. Drag the word Inserts to the Browser to save complete chains of effects. You can also add effects chains by dragging from the Browser or from the drop-down menu.

Adding Effects. Add any built-in or third-party effect by dragging it from the Browser Effects tab. Alternatively, click on the Plus icon to browse and select effects.

Figure 14-9

Power On/Off. The blue power button to the right of the word "Inserts" is used to take all the effects in the list offline. This allows you to easily go back and forth between having your mastering effects engaged and disabled.

Master Effects Inserts

The Master section follows the processing for the Track. The Master section includes two additional Insert areas: Inserts, which comes before the fader, and Post, which comes after the fader.

Figure 14-10

Post is most commonly used for adding a post level meter or a dithering plug-in. Studio One takes care of dithering seamlessly in the background if you don't worry about it, but if you want to use a specific dithering plug-in, insert it in Post and disable auto-dithering.

Effects applied at the master level are applied to all the Tracks, so your Tracks need to be well balanced in volume. The master effects you apply should provide the final touches of unifying compression and final loudness maximizing.

Selecting Monitor Outputs

Just below the Post section there is the hardware output selection. You can select any of the output pairs from your audio interface. If you have different sets of studio monitors, you can change the output pair right here and then quickly audition on two different types of speakers.

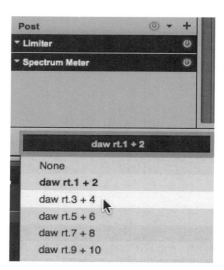

Figure 14-11

Spectrum Meter Display

The Spectrum Meter display takes up about a quarter of the Project page in the upper right quadrant of the window. It shows a visual distribution of the frequency response of the sound on playback.

Just under the Spectrum Meter display on the right, you will find the Hold and the Average controls. Hold determines how long peaks stay onscreen, with the options of None, Short, Medium, Long, and Infinity. I usually find Short to be the most useful of these options. Average determines how the averages are calculated for RMS with options of None, Fast, Medium, and Slow. At the Slow setting, it gives you a general idea of the perceived volume level of the track.

Below the Spectrum Meter display to the left are three options that determine the width of the spectrum bands, you see the following:

Octave. The Octave option breaks the frequency into octave bands. This gives you a good, rough idea of the overall song and lets you compare the frequency balance from track to track. That can give you an idea of what corrections you should make.

3rd Oct. This option shows 1/3rd-octave bands, for a bit more resolution and a finer look at the frequency response.

FFT. FFT stands for "fast Fourier transform." It is a fundamental digital signal processing calculation to break a signal into frequency components. The result in this case is a very high-resolution breakdown of the frequency response of the Track.

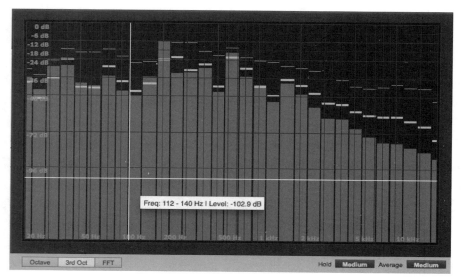

Figure 14-12

Level Meter Display

The Level Meter display is just below the Spectrum Meter display and includes options for peak/RMS modes along with full support of the K-System. Keep in mind that you can use any plug-in meters you have by inserting them in the Post area of the master.

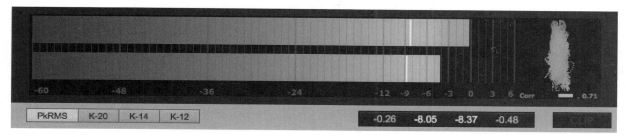

Figure 14-13

Choose PkRMS for standard mastering meters, using the buttons below the meter. As you compare Track to Track, you can target a level around which you're going to try to balance. For example, I often use –16 dB initially, then apply the master compression and limiting to match the style of music. Right-click on the meters to see additional meter options:

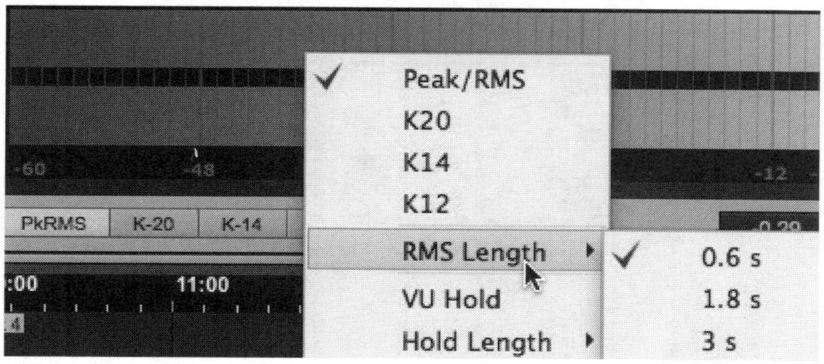

Figure 14-14

RMS Length. Set the RMS length for the meters independently from the Spectrum Meter display. The options are 0.6s, 1.8s, and 3s. The higher this is set, the slower the RMS indicator will move.

VU Hold. This holds the peaks for a while, making it easier to see the peaks.

Hold Length. Hold length is a modifier for VU hold. This sets how peaks are held before resetting. The options are 2s, 15s, and Infinity.

K-System Metering. As an alternative to typical peak RMS metering, Studio One supports the K-System, which I will explain in the next section.

K-System Metering

Modern pop songs tend to be released with very loud mastering. If you play a reference tune back, you often find the RMS level hovering around –6 dB. Many users have complained that mixes mastered this way have limited dynamic range and sound distorted. That's where the K-System comes in.

Figure 14-15

Instead of mixing and mastering to full scale, the K-System brings the zero dB reference level down to leave more headroom. The K-System features three different meter types calibrated to different applications: K-12 is for broadcast, K-14 is for pop music, and K-20 is for orchestral music.

Another component of the K-System encourages you to calibrate your speakers to a fixed loudness at the mix position. If you are serious about using the K-System, you can get more information online (Figure 14-15).

The reality is that commercial releases are much hotter than any of these. All of the engineers that I know who use the K-System mix music to K-12, and then follow that with additional mastering. This is all about to change with new broadcast standards rolling out in Europe and the US that will allow for more dynamic range by automatically leveling the volume of playback. The "Sound Check" setting in iTunes currently does the same thing, but it is turned off by default. My new approach is to mix with K-20 and master with K-14.

Project Page Timeline

Until now, we have been focusing on the Track List but the Timeline is an essential tool as well. Here are key things you can do from this view:

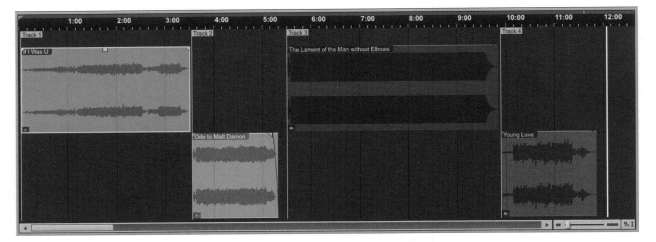

Figure 14-16

Drag and Drop. You can drag Studio One Song files to the Timeline and drop them right in the position that you want them. You can also import other types of audio files from your computer by just dragging them from your desktop or the Browser. To change the order of the Tracks, use the Track List.

Loop In / Out. Draw in the loop on the upper part of the Timeline just like you do in the Arrange view. You can enable or disable the loop in the Transport or using the forward slash (/) key.

Zooming In / Out. Zoom in and out with W and E on keyboard, just as you did in the Song page. Zoom controls and Data Zoom are in the lower right and work the same as always.

Index Markers. Studio One automatically adds Track Markers at the start of each Track. You can also add Index Markers within a Track. To do this, move the mouse pointer to the top of the Track area in the Timeline until the pointer turns into a pencil shape. Click on where you want the Index Marker to be. Right-click on an Index Marker to delete it.

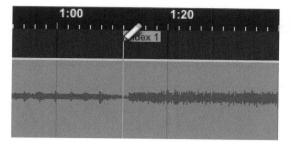

Figure 14-17

Splitting a Track. If you have more than one song on a Track, you probably want to split so it appears as two different Tracks on your album. You might also have a concert recording with an entire concert that you want to divide into the individual Tracks.

Fortunately, it is very easy to split Tracks. Place the cursor where you want to make the split, right-click on the Track, and select Split at Cursor, or hit Opt + X / Alt + X.

Track-to-Track Crossfades. You can easily drag tracks in the Timeline so that they overlap, since the Tracks alternate between two different lanes. However, to fade in the next Track as the previous fades out, you need to create a crossfade.

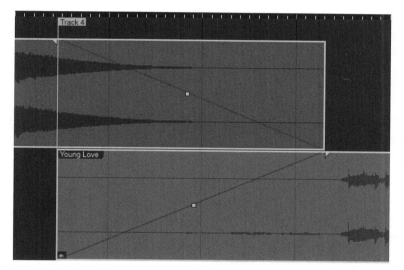

Figure 14-18

To crossfade, select both Tracks and hit X. Use the handles on the fade envelope to adjust the fades just like you would for Events on the Song page.

Understand that a crossfade is really going to mix the overlapped part into the later Track. If you plan to export the album as MP3 files, you're going to hear a fade-out if you play the Track alone.

Using this sort of crossfade is not nearly as useful now that most distribution is done with digital releases. Consider creating different versions for MP3 and CD if you must use Track-to-Track crossfades.

Project Transport

The Transport area at the bottom of the Project page is a simplified version of the Transport area from the Song page.

Figure 14-19

The basic transport controls are all here, minus the things that don't apply to Projects. Here are a few things to pay attention to:

Time Display Modes. Click below the time readout to select the units from seconds, samples, bars, and frames. I find frames or seconds to be the most useful. Note that frames mode still shows hours, minutes, and seconds. It's just that the subsecond times are divided into frames in what is essentially a timecode.

Fader and Meter. The Meter section in the Transport bar is a small version of the master meter. If you drag this, the master fader actually changes. This can really upset carefully balanced master setups, so be careful! Honestly, this is not the best way to adjust the master volume.

Stereo/Mono. You can flip the output to mono using the Stereo/Mono icon. In mono mode it appears as bright red, which is good because it's obvious. You don't want to accidentally export your release in mono.

Mastering Steps

Mastering involves several processes that usually include volume, leveling, EQ, compression, and preparation for releasing. This is a very short summary of the mastering steps I use in Studio One.

1. **Track-to-Track Volume Leveling.** Listen back and check Track-to-Track volumes. Adjust them to match using the Track faders. If a Track is too far out from the other Tracks, open the Song mix and make the changes there. This is easy because Studio One will prompt you to resync the mastering files when you come back to the Project page. At this point, I will do several checks just dropping the cursor in various locations within the Tracks.

   If you want, you can use the loudness detection tool to see how the mixes compare and make mix volume tweaks before applying any of the mastering effects.

2. **Track EQ.** Pro EQ is a great tool to make minor corrections or enhancements to each track. I usually apply EQ separately to each Track, and then listen to make sure each Track matches. If I find I need to add too much EQ, I would rather open the Song file and tweak the mix rather than use too much correction at this stage. You can add many other kinds of effects and compression here if you want, but basic EQ should be added very sparingly.

3. **Track Compression.** Using this is optional, but if you want to start to bring the level up, it is better to do this in multiple small stages rather than all at once. Compressor or Tricomp are good tools for this.

4. **Master Compression.** Volumes have been written on how to use mastering compression. Compressor and the Tricomp work great. I like to run them both and have each do a little bit of compression. It is common in mastering to do light gain reduction in several stages rather than apply any one tool aggressively.

   Studio One also has the comprehensive Multiband compressor. Multiband compression can be a great tool if used carefully, but it's easy to do more harm than good. I tend to save it for repairing mix problems.

5. **Loudness Maximizing.** To finalize the tracks to commercial quality you might want to employ a third-party tool like Slate FGX, Waves L2, or Izotope Ozone. I typically put a maximizer plug-in into the Post section of the master, so that it is at the very end of the audio path.

6. **Limiting.** If you aren't using a loudness maximizer, then you can use the Limiter effect as the final stage. It is a good practice to set this at about −0.3 dB and engage the ISL option. That gives you just a bit of headroom to reduce the chance of intersample peaks causing distortion on playback.

   The Threshold control brings on a 20:1 ratio compression, so setting that below the ceiling can also help. I use that as a final safety net.

7. **Dithering.** To keep things simple, don't worry about dithering. Studio One takes care of it behind the scenes transparently. Just make sure to disable any dithering that might be added by third-party plug-ins.

   If you want to use third-party dithering, then disable dithering in Options and insert the dithering plug-in in the Post bin.

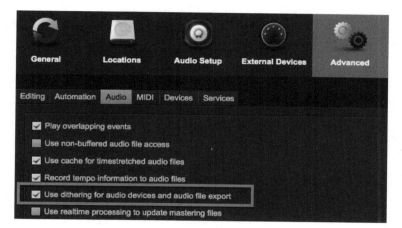

Figure 14-20

Tip: Once you have a mastering chain you like, drag it to the Browser for use on your next project.

Chapter 15
RELEASING

Authoring Red Book CDs

Once you can play back a project and be happy with the way it sounds, the actual mastering and releasing is very easy. In this chapter, I will go over the steps and options for each possible kind of release.

Burning a CD Master

To burn a CD, click on the Burn icon in the Toolbar. If you have multiple CD drives, you can choose which one to use. Choose the speed. Many engineers assume that the slowest speed will give you the best quality, but for quick scratch masters or to listen on your car stereo, you can speed it up.

If you choose to do a test write, it won't actually burn the CD, but will test to see if the burn will work. Burn Proof is a feature of some CD burners. If you turn this on, it will attempt to use that feature in the hardware to reduce creating bad discs.

If you choose to use a temporary image file, Studio One creates a complete image file of the disc before burning it. I think this is a very good idea, especially if you have a slower computer. Theoretically, it makes the CD-creation process more reliable.

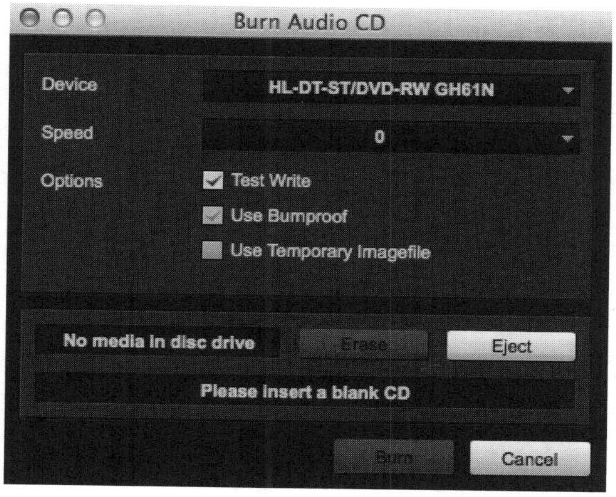

The Burn dialog box also shows the media type. If it an erasable disc, you can erase it here. There is also an Eject option.

Figure 15-1

Once you have the options set correctly and a blank CD is loaded, click on Burn. In a few minutes the CD will be done. The time depends on the speed you selected for burning and the speed of your computer.

Making a Disc Image

An ISO disc image consists of two files: one continuous WAV file that includes the audio for the entire CD, and a text file that lists the cue points defining where each Track starts. Disc image files are used by other CD-burning software and manufacturing houses to create CDs.

You can use this in the event you're having some trouble burning good CDs with your computer. Create an ISO disc image, then use one of the dedicated CD-burning programs that will burn from an ISO image.

To create an image, click on the Image icon on the Toolbar to open the Make Image dialog box. There are a few options in the dialog box:

Location. Location is where you can find the image on your system when it's done. By default it goes to the Studio One Projects folder and into a subfolder that is automatically created.

Format. You can select to output the image in a variety of formats: WAV, AIFF, FLAC, Ogg Vorbis, or MP3. Normally, WAV is the most common format used for this. However, if you are creating a podcast and want a full-length file to upload, then MP3 would be the typical choice.

Realtime Processing. This option renders the image in real time. This is necessary only if you are running through external hardware via the Pipeline plug-in.

Upload to SoundCloud. This option will load the rendered file into the SoundCloud client for easy upload. I would rarely do this with the full image and would usually use Digital Release instead.

Figure 15-2

Image files appear in the Project folder structure in the Releases subfolder. Here you will find the exported audio file. The file name will match the Project name, along with an appropriate extension based on the format (for example, .WAV). You will also find a similarly named cue sheet file with a .TXT extension.

DDP Exports

DDP stands for Disc Description Protocol. This is specifically for sending to disc-manufacturing houses. Click on DDP and you get a single option asking if you want to create a DDP image. Click on Yes and the rest happens automatically. It takes several minutes, depending on the length of the project.

Studio One

Do you want to create a DDP image?

Image: Rhyme Without Reason
Location: /Volumes/Glyph/Studio One/Projects/
Rhyme Without Reason

No   Yes

Figure 15-3

When it's finished, look for the output in the Project folder. You will see a new folder that starts with the Project name and ends with DDP. This folder contains several DDP documents. Send the entire folder to your disc manufacturer. Usually, you'll want to compress it into a Zip file first.

Digital Releases

I find the Digital Release option gets the most use. This allows you to create individual MP3 files for each track. You can release all the files or just pick from some of them. You can also release in any supported format. Releasing WAV files with minimal processing is also a good idea if you are having mastering done by someone else.

Releasing MP3 Tracks

Click on Digital Release in the Toolbar, and the Digital Release dialog box will come up. This is very similar to the other Export dialog boxes. There are options for naming the files with Track numbers and the artist name. To release MP3s, select MP3 and the bit rate in the Format section.

On the left side you can choose to remove some of the Tracks if you don't want to release them all. Click on OK to render the files. The files will appear in the Releases subfolder for the Project.

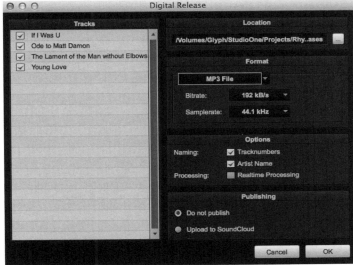

Releasing WAV Files

Releasing WAV files works exactly the same way as releasing MP3 files, except you need to select Wave File in the Format section and set Resolution to the correct bit depth. For CDs, set it to 16-bit. If the files will move on to mastering, leave them set at the Project bit depth.

Figure 15-4

Concluding Remarks

That brings us to the end of this book. It's impossible to provide absolutely comprehensive coverage of any modern DAW in a Quick Pro book. I have made my best effort to cover the key topics so you can get going with Studio One quickly.

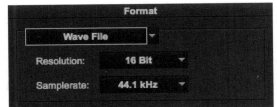

Figure 15-5

I think you will find Studio One to be easy to use. Many report that it provides a fun, uncluttered UI to create with. The innovative features and workflow might be pretty exciting because they inspire thoughts about the potential of DAWs in the future, but the real joy comes from creating new music. That's what inspired the guys at PreSonus to create Studio One in the first place.

APPENDIX: ABOUT THE DVD-ROM

Media

The DVD-ROM included with this book contains a number of video tutorials designed to help you understand the features and techniques explained in *Studio One for Engineers and Producers*. Use these videos to learn more about the Studio One environment and to gain greater understanding of the processes described in the text.

1. External Device Setup

This video covers the basics of connecting external MIDI keyboards and control surfaces to Studio One.

2. Recording to Layers

In this video I demonstrate recording to layers by looping them using keyboard shortcuts.

3. Setting the Tempo of Imported Audio

Learn how to drag audio files into a Song and make sure the tempo is correct so that timestretching works right.

4. Comping Example

See how to build a composite solo line from takes.

5. Audio Bend Examples

Watch examples of using Audio Bend by placing Bend Markers manually and with transient detection.

6. Audio Parts

Learn how to create and work with events made up of slices of audio.

7. Groove Quantize Examples

See how to use Groove Quantize to set the quantize grid to match and existing track, then quantize to impart the groove to other tracks.

8. Multitrack Audio Bend

Learn how to correct the timing of multitrack drums without adding phase problems.

9. Control Link Demo

See how to use Control Link to map a MIDI controller to onscreen controls.

10. Melodyne Main Tool

See how to invoke Melodyne to edit audio and how to use the Main tool to tweak pitch and timing.

11. Project Page Sync to Song Page

Learn how the Project page mastering files relate to Song page mixes.

12. Macro Toolbar

An introduction and a few examples for using and creating macros in Studio One.

Keyboard Shortcuts by Chapter

What follows are lists of the keyboard shortcuts referenced by chapter. They are supplied here and also included on the DVD-ROM as a PDF that you can print and keep close by at all times.

Chapter 1: Getting Started

Play/Stop	Spacebar
Return to Zero	Comma
Forward	Numpad +
Rewind	Numpad −
Zoom In Horizontal	E
Zoom Out Horizontal	W
Zoom In Vertical	Shift + E
Zoom Out Vertical	Shift + W
Set the Loop over Event	select event and press P
Zoom to the Loop	Shift + L
Undo	Cmd + Z / Ctrl + Z

Chapter 2: Songs

Save	Cmd + S / Ctrl + S
Quantize	Q
Snap Mode On/Off	N

Chapter 3: Tracks

Place Marker at Cursor	Y
Place Named Marker at Cursor	Shift + Y
Go to Next Marker	Shift + N
Go to Previous Marker	Shift + B
Add Track	T
Mute	M
Solo	S
Input Monitor	U
Group Selected Tracks	Cmd + G / Ctrl + G
Dissolve Group	Shift + Cmd + G / Shift + Ctrl + G

Chapter 4: Recording Audio

Enable Preroll	O
Arm Tracks	R
Start Recording	Numpad *
Activate Loop Mode	/
Activate Auto Punch	I (capital letter "i")

Chapter 5: Editing Audio

Snap Mode On/Off	N
Duplicate	D
Duplicate Shared	Shift + D
Duplicate and Insert	Opt + D / Alt + D
Open Editor	F2
Slip Event	Opt + Cmd + Drag / Ctrl + Alt + Drag
Arrow Tool	1
Range Tool	2
Split Tool	3
Eraser Tool	4
Paint Tool	5
Mute Tool	6
Bend Tool	7
Listen Tool	8
Create Crossfade	X
Place Cursor at Mouse Pointer	Cmd + Spacebar / Ctrl + Spacebar
Split Event at Cursor	Opt + X / Alt + X
Move Cursor to Next Transient	Tab
Bounce Selected Events	Cmd + B / Ctrl + B

Chapter 6: Audio Bend and Quantize

Move Bend Marker	Opt + Drag / Alt + Drag
Quantize Selected Events	Q
Bounce Selected Events	Cmd + B / Ctrl + B

Chapter 7: Melodyne Integration

Open Melodyne View	Cmd + M / Ctrl + M
Remove Melodyne from Event	Opt + Cmd + M / Alt + Ctrl + M
Select All	Cmd + A / Ctrl + A

Chapter 8: Instrument Parts and Virtual Instruments (MIDI)

Bounce Instrument Parts	Cmd + B / Ctrl + B
Group Selected Tracks	Cmd + G / Ctrl + G
Dissolve Group	Shift + Cmd + G / Shift + Ctrl + G
Duplicate	D
Duplicate Shared	Shift + D
Paint Tool	5
Open Editor	F2
Enable Auto Scroll	F
Quantize	Q
Restore Timing	Shift + Q

Chapter 9: The Studio One Console

Open Console View	F3
Group Selected Tracks	Cmd + G / Ctrl + G
Dissolve Group	Shift + Cmd + G / Shift + Ctrl + G
Move Channel Selection Forward	]
Move Channel Selection Backward	[

Chapter 10: Working with Effects

Open Browser with Effects Tab Selected	F7
Open Search Bar	Cmd + F / Ctrl + F
Open Effect Window for Currently Selected Channel	F11
Cycle Through Tabs of Effect Window	Cmd + PageDn or Cmd + PageUp / Ctrl + PageDn or Ctrl + PageUp

Chapter 11: Essential Built-In Effects

None

Chapter 12: Automation

Open Options Dialog	Cmd + Comma / Ctrl + Comma
Enable Show Automation	A
Reset a Node to the Default Value	Cmd-click / Ctrl-click

Chapter 13: Mixing and Exporting

Bounce Selection	Cmd + B / Ctrl + B
Create Audio Part from Selection	G
Duplicate	D
Duplicate Shared	Shift + D
Open Export Stems Dialog Box	Shift + Cmd + E / Shift + Ctrl + E
Select All Events	Cmd + A / Ctrl + A
Set Loop over Selection	P

Chapter 14: The Project Page

Enable/Disable Loop	/
Zoom In	W
Zoom Out	E
Split at Cursor	Opt + X / Alt + X
Crossfade Selection	X

Chapter 15: Releasing

None

INDEX